RIGHT DOWN YOUR ALLEY:
The Complete Book of Bowling

Dedication

We dedicate this book to our parents.

Published by Leisure Press
A division of Human Kinetics Publishers, Inc.
Box 5076
Champaign, IL 61825-5076
1-800-747-4457

UK Office:
Human Kinetics Publishers (UK) Ltd.
P.O. Box 18
Rawdon, Leeds LS19 6TG
England
(0532) 504211

Library of Congress Cataloging in Publication Data

Grinfelds, Vesma.
    Right down your alley.

    1. Bowling. I. Hultstrand, Bonnie II. Title.
GV903.G74   1985   794.6   84-12601
ISBN 0-88011-252-2

RIGHT DOWN YOUR ALLEY

The Complete Book of Bowling

2ND EDITION

Vesma Grinfelds
Master Clinician
National Bowling Council

Bonnie Hultstrand
University of Idaho

LEISURE PRESS
Champaign, Illinois

Contents

Acknowledgments

The authors wish to extend their sincere gratitude to the many friends who have helped make this book possible. We thank Kathy Clark and Dorothy Zakrajsek for the constant encouragement and patient assistance in editing the manuscript; Karen Gantz and Launa Morasch for their unending hours in preparing the manuscript; Louis Henning Kahn for the hours spent in providing the fine photographs; Ben H. Womack for his dedicated efforts in creating the illustrations; to the many students who unselfishly gave of their time in many ways; and Cindy Petrucek, David Kappel, Fran Person and Ben Falzone who so willingly gave of their time to be subjects for the photographs. We would also like to express our appreciation to the National Bowling Council for providing us with many of the illustrations and information. To all of you, we are deeply indebted!

Preface

All sporting activities have gone through great changes in recent years due to additional research and experimentation. Bowling is no exception. It is our intent to present in this book the newest, proven bowling techniques of our time. Many concepts included in this text have never been in print before, and yet are used universally by expert bowlers. The material presented is the amalgamation of the experience of both authors, one as a teacher and coach, and the other as a professional bowler and clinician.

We have attempted to show that bowling should have a high degree of natural feeling involved in the movement pattern. Complimenting this naturalness is the integration of efficient movement principles for accuracy and consistency.

This text includes everything a bowler, whether beginner or advanced, needs to know about the game of bowling in order to keep improving. In addition to the basics of bowling, we have included an advanced bowling section for those who are past the novice stage. We have also devoted a chapter to the competitive aspects of bowling and ideas on how to coach a bowler.

Through our efforts, we hope we can give each reader a better understanding of the elements involved in the game of bowling and enhance his/her enjoyment and performance in the number one indoor participant sport in the United States.

Vesma Grinfelds
Bonnie Hultstrand

PART A
BASIC BOWLING

The modern form of bowling at pins probably originated in ancient Germany, not as a sport but as a religious ceremony.

1

History of Bowling

Bowling may very well be the oldest form of recreation in the world today. An ancient version of a ball and pins resembling the current day bowling equipment was found in an Egyptian child's grave dating back to approximately 5200 B.C. More than likely the Stone Age man may have enjoyed rolling rocks at other rocks. We know the ancient Polynesians played a game resembling bowling in which they used pins and balls made of stone and rolled the balls a distance similar to the length of the present lane bed.

It has also been recorded that about the time of Christ, rolling rocks down hills was a form of war maneuver used to bowl the enemy over with a strike. This skill was practiced by the soldiers in order to develop accuracy and before long they found it to be a form of play. The Italian game of *bocce,* (which is still widely played among persons of Italian descent), probably originated from this early war game.

The modern form of bowling at pins probably originated in ancient Germany, not as a sport but as a religious ceremony. The parishioner would bring his *"kegel"* and place at the end of a cloister in the cathedral. He was then given a round stone to roll at the *kegel* which represented *"heide,"* the heathen. If the parishioner was successful in knocking down the *kegel,* he was to have cleansed himself of sin. According to a nineteenth century German historian, Wilhelm Pehle, this religious ceremony had it origin as early as the third or four century, and lasted less than two centuries.

As time passed, the game of bowling evolved into a recreational pastime rather than a religious ceremony. Martin Luther is said to have enjoyed the game of bowling and built a bowling lane for the younger members of his family. He is also credited with establishing the first set of rules for ninepin bowling. In ninepin, the pins were set in a diamond shape with the kingpin in the middle. The object was to knock down as many pins as possible without spilling the kingpin.

The game of ninepin was the form of bowling which was brought to America by the Dutch early in the seventeenth century. One of the early playing areas was in lower Manhattan, the spot still known as Bowling Green.

The game of bowling flourished in America and spread throughout the states. By the mid 1830's, it became a gambling sport which led to legislation banning ninepins in the 1840's. In order to circumvent the legislation, a tenth pin was added and all of the pins were placed in an equilateral triangle.

The new tenpin game did suffer in some areas from gambling but the biggest hindrance was the lack of uniform rules and equipment specifications. In 1895, the American Bowling Congress (ABC) was organized to standardize the playing rules and regulations. By the early 1900's, women became very interested in the game of bowling and formed their own organization to standardize rules and sponsor competition. The Women's National Bowling Association, today known as the Women's International Bowling Congress (WIBC), was formed in 1916.

Another stabilizing influence came in 1932 with the formation of the Bowling Proprietors Association of America (BPAA). This organization was designed to improve the management of the sport and to stimulate the growth of bowling throughout the country through promotion programs and tournament sponsorship.

During World War II, bowling became a widespread recreational sport. It was one of the leisure activities provided by the armed forces for the many soldiers in training as well as for wounded veterans. In 1943, the National Bowling Council (NBC) was formed to coordinate all phases of bowling in the war effort. After the war, NBC became an informational clearing house and legislative liaison organization for the sport. Today, the NBC serves as national coordinator for the sport of bowling.

Bowling attracts millions of participants. With the addition of new, attractive bowling centers with automatic pinsetting machines, bowling has become a family sport. By 1970, the nation's most popular indoor participation sport was being enjoyed by nearly 52 million Americans of all ages.

2

Understanding The Basics

On the surface, the game of bowling appears quite simple. The bowler takes an approach, rolls a fairly heavy ball down a 60 foot lane, and with two attempts tries to knock down the ten wooden pins placed in a triangular fashion at the end of the lane. However, as the bowler delves into the mechanics of bowling, he/she finds a much more complicated game.

It is true that each bowler establishes his/her own style. However, truly successful bowlers seem to have many attributes in common: (1) They all have a smooth, flowing approach and delivery; (2) they all have excellent timing, balance, and flexibility during the approach and delivery; (3) their swing and approach is absolutely consistent on each delivery; (4) they have complete concentration, poise, and confidence; (5) and each has developed a system of adjustment to assist in compensating for varying lane conditions. These things do not just happen. They are practiced, thought through, and then grooved to the extent of becoming automatic.

The key to success in bowling lies in knowing the game inside and out and being able to groove the entire approach, swing, and delivery where consistency is an absolute.

In the following chapters, we intend to present all of the information necessary for a bowler to achieve his/her potential. The material presented has been tried and proven by the best in the world.

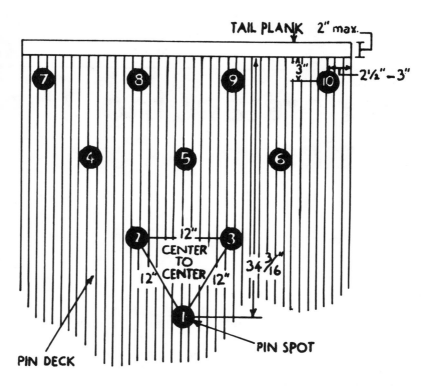

Figure 2.1 In an ABC regulation bowling lane the pins are arranged in a 35-inch equilateral triangle. Each pin is 12 inches from the adjacent pin, center to center. (Courtesy of NBC)

FEATURES OF BALL, PINS AND LANES

Understanding ball, lane, and pin composition and dimensions will aid the bowler in grasping the mechanical and mathematical concepts involved in bowling.

Bowling Ball

Bowling balls range from eight to sixteen pounds in weight and are constructed of hard rubber or a synthetic plastic material. The number of finger holes in the ball vary from two to five, but the ball with three finger holes is the most common. No matter what the weight, the ball measures approximately 27 inches in circumference and about 8 1/2 inches in diameter.

Bowling Pins

Bowling pins are made of durable materials, usually hard rock maple covered by a thin plastic coating. They are 15 inches in height and 15 inches in circumference around the belly of the pin. The diameter is approximately 4 3/4 inches through the widest part. According to the American Bowling Congress (ABC), pins may be no lighter than three pounds six ounces, and no heavier than three pounds ten ounces. Furthermore, the set of pins in service at an establishment must all be of the same weight. On the bottom of the pin there is a nylon cap to protect it from wear and tear. Taking these specifications into consideration, it is interesting to note that a pin will topple when it moves 10 degrees off its vertical axis.

There are ten pins set on the lane in a 36-inch equilateral triangle with each pin around the perimeter of the triangle and across the rows spread 12 inches apart, center to center. (Figure 2.1)

In examining the ball dimensions in relation to the pins, it is found that a single pin left standing could be contacted by the ball anywhere within a 21-inch area. It should also be noted that a ball cannot pass directly between two pins without contacting one or both of them. (Figure 2.2)

The pins are numbered from front to back, always starting from left and going to the right. Before proceeding, the reader must memorize the pins by their correct number.

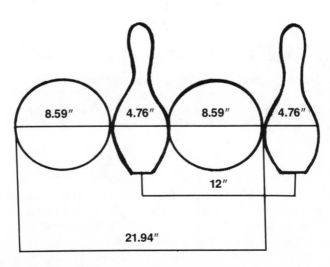

Figure 2.2 Relative dimensions of ball and pins.

SELF EVALUATION QUESTIONS

1. How many inches apart are the pins located?
2. Number the pins.

Lane Features and Dimensions

In order for a bowler to understand the bulk of material yet to be presented in this text, it is imperative to understand and be able to identify the different parts of the lane and its dimensions.

The bowling area is divided into four segments—the approach, the lane, the pin deck, and the pit area.

The Approach

The approach is the area found toward the back of the lane where bowlers take their steps and swing prior to the delivery of the ball. The approach is made up of laminated boards which are a little over an inch in width and about four inches thick, set on end. These boards match the 39 boards which make up the lane in front of the approach area.

Usually on this approach, a bowler may identify three rows of dots extending parallel to the foul line. These dots are known as locator dots and are used by bowlers in finding their proper stance. The first row of locator dots can be found two to three inches behind the foul line. The other two rows are found 12 and 15 feet, respectively, from the foul line. The dots are equally placed five boards apart and the center dot is in the center of the approach which corresponds to the 20th board in the center of the lane.

SELF EVALUATION QUESTIONS

1. How many boards make up a bowling lane?
2. How many boards apart are the locator dots placed?
3. What is the minimum length of a bowling approach?

The Lane

The lane is the area in front of the approach and foul line where the ball rolls to encounter the pins. The width of the lane is approximately 42 inches made up of the 39 laminated boards slightly over an inch in width plus a narrower filler board usually found somewhere between the edge board and first arrow on the left.

The length of the lane from the foul line to the center of the head pin is 60 feet. (Figure 2.3) The first one-third of the lane, plus the outside

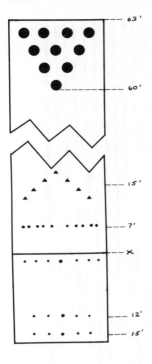

Figure 2.3 Relative distance of lane and approach markings from the foul line.

board, and the area under the pins is constructed of hard maple which is extremely durable. The remainder of the lane to the head pin is constructed of pine. Since pine is much softer and grainier, it assists the bowling ball in "grabbing" the lane, resulting in greater hooking action.

On the lane area, we find seven large markings placed in an inverted V formation, known as target arrows. These target arrows have special significance to each bowler. They help bowlers to focus on a specific target while delivering the ball, a procedure known as spot bowling. These target arrows are located 15 feet from the foul line with the center arrow on the 20th baord. Just as on the approach, these arrows are also spaced five boards apart so that the third arrow from the right corresponds with the 15th board, the second arrow is on the 10th board, and the first arrow is located on the 5th board. (Please note: Left-handers number these target arrows from left to right.) (Figure 2.4)

Halfway between the foul line and the target arrows there is a row of dots called the spots. These spots are *not* lined up with the other locator dots or target arrows and are of little or no use to the average bowler. The spots are only of value to higher average bowlers, those who are extremely nearsighted, or those who have physical handicaps.

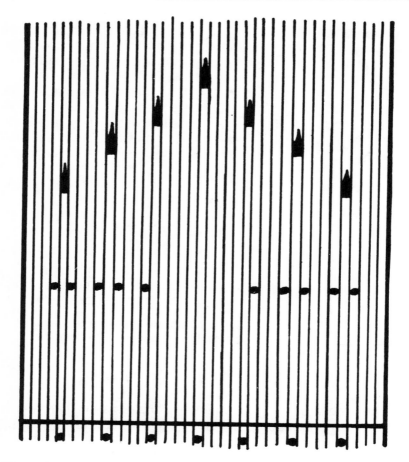

Figure 2.4 The target arrows and locator dots on the approach are each located on every fifth board. They do not coincide with the spots in between the foul line and the target arrows. (Courtesy of NBC)

SELF EVALUATION QUESTIONS

1. How many boards apart are the target arrows?
2. Are they in line with the locator dots on the approach?
3. How many boards make up the width of a lane?
4. How far is it from the foul line to the head pin?

The Pin Deck and Pit Area

The area of the lane where the pins are set is called the pin deck. It is approximately 36 inches in depth and is made of hardwood and durable synthetic materials to take the wear and tear of falling and flying pins.

To the sides of the pin deck are side partitions called kickbacks which help contain the pins and assist pin action on the pin deck. These kickbacks span the entire area from opposite the head pin to the rear cushion found above the pit area.

The pit area is approximately 4 3/4 inches below the surface of the pin deck and extends another 30 inches back to the cushion. This area is recessed in order to catch the pins before they have a chance to bounce back out on the lane. It usually contains a moveable belt that carries the ball back to the ball return and the pins into the automatic pinsetter.

ETIQUETTE AND SAFETY

There are many commonly accepted rules of etiquette that everyone should follow upon entering the bowling establishment. By using common sense and following these basic rules of etiquette, we will assist the management in keeping maintenance costs down, be respected and appreciated by others on the lanes, and help make the game of bowling pleasant and safe for all.

Basic Rules of Etiquette and Safety

- Before stepping onto the lane, check to make sure the bowlers on the adjoining lanes are not in their stance or taking their approach. The rule is: ONLY ONE PERSON ON THE APPROACH AT THE SAME TIME. If you both step up on the approach at the same time, YIELD TO THE PERSON ON THE RIGHT.
- Bowling is a sport which requires intense concentration. Therefore, refrain from disturbing any bowler in his/her approach. Loud noises and constant movement are very distracting to all.
- Restrict your body english and confine your elation or disappointment to your own lane or within yourself. Kicking the ball return or other equipment doesn't help anyone.
- After you have delivered the ball, walk straight back and step off the approach while waiting for the return of the ball.
- Take a *reasonable* amount of time while on the approach area but think of others. Many people become irritated if they have to wait too long for someone else.
- Use only *your* ball, towel, resin and other equipment unless you have permission to borrow someone else's.
- Keep refreshments out of the bowler's settee area. Spilled liquids present problems to all bowlers.
- Be prepared to bowl when it is your turn. Plan your absences from the lane so no one will have to wait for you to return.

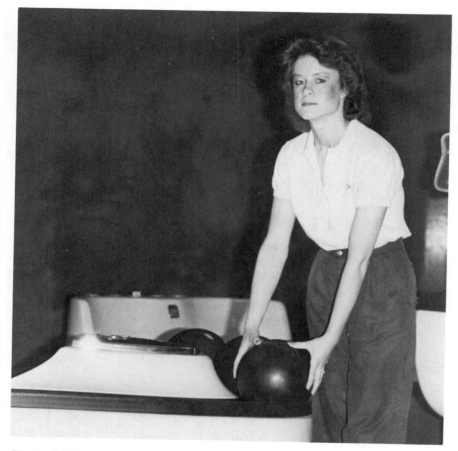

Figure 2.5 The proper way to remove a ball from the ball racks minimizing the chances of hand or finger injury.

- Change into your bowling shoes before entering the bowling area. This will keep the area free from mud, water, and dirt which may be picked up by bowler's shoes and carried onto the lanes.
- Refrain from blaming someone else or equipment for your mistakes. More than likely it is your fault when things go wrong.
- Refrain from giving advice to others unless they ask for your help.
- Make sure the ball sweep is up before you deliver the ball.
- Accept defeat gracefully and winning modestly.
- Avoid lofting the ball. This is damaging to the lanes as well as distracting to others.
- Avoid wearing long skirts or pants and floppy sleeves which may get tangled during the approach and cause a mishap.

- When lifting your bowling ball back from the rack, to avoid pinched fingers and back strain, place both hands on each side of the ball, bend your knees, and lift by straightening the legs. (Figure 2.5)

By following these simple rules, bowling will be more enjoyable to all. Remember the basic rule of good manners: BE CONSIDERATE OF OTHERS.

BEFORE YOU START BOWLING, YOU SHOULD KNOW:

- In order to become a good bowler you must groove the approach, the swing, and the delivery.
- The bowling pins are set in a precise 36 inch equilateral triangle; are spaced 12 inches apart from center to center; and are numbered from left to right.
- The head pin is located on the 20th board and is 60 feet from the foul line.
- The approach is a minimum of 15 feet in length and has three sets of locator dots.
- The locator dots are spaced 5 boards apart with the center dot on the 20th board. The dots and boards are always counted from the outside edge of the lane toward the center.
- The target arrows used for aiming in spot bowling are 15 feet in front of the foul line. They are also spaced 5 boards apart and are in direct line with the locator dots on the approach.
- The basic rule of etiquette and safety involves being considerate of others.

Remember the basic rule of good manners. BE CONSIDERATE OF OTHERS.

3

Preparing For Action

SELECTION OF PROPER EQUIPMENT

Proper selection of equipment is essential for bowling success. Two basic equipment needs are a well fitted ball and a pair of bowling shoes.

Bowling Shoes

The bowling shoes rented at a bowling establishment are dual-purpose shoes that can be used by right or left-handers because both the left and right soles are made of sliding material. When renting shoes, make sure that they fit comfortably and will slide at the end of the approach.

If you are right-handed, care must be taken when purchasing a pair of bowling shoes so that the shoes are designed for right-handers. The soles of most higher quality shoes are constructed to give one foot some traction, while giving the other foot a sole for sliding purposes. Since sliding is done on the left foot for a right-handed delivery, the left sole is usually made of leather. The right foot is used for traction so the right sole of the shoe is usually rubber with a leather tip. This is reversed for left-handed bowler's shoes.

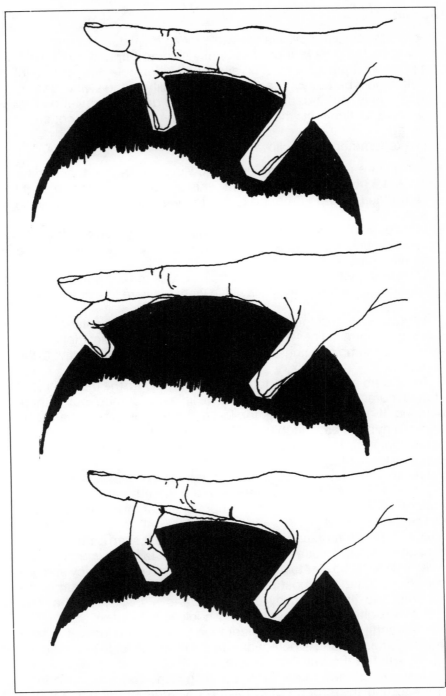

Figure 3.1 Different types of grips. a) Conventional b) Fingertip c) Semi-fingertip

Bowling Ball

To provide consistency, it is desirable for an individual to purchase a bowling ball and have it professionally selected and fitted. If this is not possible, then care must be exercised when selecting a "house" ball. It should be heavy enough to add stability to the swing, and yet not so heavy that it causes the shoulder to drop. A heavier ball will have less deflection when it hits the pins resulting in better pin coverage.

We recommend the following guidelines:

- For children under twelve, use a bowling ball that is 1 pound for every 10 pounds of body weight. This should come close to eight year olds using an 8-pound ball; a ten year old using a 10-pound ball, etc.
- Most beginning women bowlers should be able to start with an 11 or 12-pound ball and as they progress they can move up to a heavier ball.
- Most beginning male bowlers should be able to start with a 14 or 15 pounder. Eventually, they may also want to move to a heavier ball.

After attending to the weight of the ball, the next consideration is hand and finger fit. The two most important factors to consider are the size of the thumb and finger holes and the span from the thumb to the fingers.

The thumb should comfortably and snugly fit into the thumb hole. It should come out of the hole with a little resistance but without popping. If the thumb hole is too large, many problems will arise by trying to grip the ball much too tightly with the thumb joint. The finger holes should fit the fingers fairly snug and should allow the fingers to come out smoothly and without resistance.

The second important element in obtaining a proper fit is determining the span or distance between the thumb and the fingers according to the preferred grip—conventional, fingertip, or semi-fingertip (Figure 3.1)

The most common grip which has the shortest span is the conventional grip. Most "house" balls are drilled with this grip which potentially allows the bowler to develop a high degree of accuracy and ball control. The second most popular grip with the largest span is the fingertip grip. It is used by consistent and highly skilled bowlers looking to achieve a higher degree of hook power and pin action. The semi-fingertip span is slightly wider than the conventional yet shorter than the fingertip and is potentially useful for a bowler to increase the lift imparted at the point of release.

Most novice and intermediate bowlers use the conventional grip. In order to find the proper span for the conventional grip, place the thumb all the way into the thumb hole. Making sure the wrist remains

Figure 3.2 Conventional grip   **Figure 3.3 Fingertip grip**

straight, extend the fingers across the span area of the ball. The lines on the second knuckle of your middle finger should exceed the edge of the finger hole closest to the thumb by about 1/4 of an inch. (Figure 3.2).

The second most popular bowling grip is the fingertip. Since the span is wider in this fingertip than in the conventional grip, measurement is made by using the first joint of the fingers instead of the second joint as in the conventional grip. To find the proper fit for the fingertip ball, place the thumb all the way in the thumb hole and extend the fingers over the surface of the ball. The line of the first joint will land right in the middle of the fingerhole. If the ball fits correctly with the thumb and fingers in the ball, the second knuckle should be sticking up in the air slightly and forming a little triangle. (Figure 3.3). If it is flat against the surface of the ball, the span is too long and the evidence will be burnt fingertips or excessive callouses. To insure a properly drilled fingertip ball, a professional driller in a reputable pro shop should be sought.

In comparing the advantages and disadvantages of the afore-mentioned conventional and fingertip grips, one finds that neither is perfect. Of the two, the conventional grip probably helps develop greater accuracy. The major disadvantage is that the hooking action is only minimal because so much of the hand is inside the ball. The thumb comes out first, but, due to the compactness of the fingers, not enough time elapses for proper hand action to take place. This results in reduced hooking action with less pin carry.

The fingertip ball may be less accurate than the conventional grip but has a greater pin carry due to an increased hooking action. This greater hooking action is a result of greater lift and more revolutions that can be imparted on the ball with the wider span.

The third type of grip called the semi-fingertip was designed to combine the advantages of both the conventional and fingertip—the control and accuracy of the conventional and the extra hooking action of the fingertip. The span is equidistant between the two first joints of the fingers. This particular grip has been found unsatisfactory primarily because the fingers cannot bend at the location between the two joints. This causes the fingers to grip the back of the hole and often causes discomfort to the bowler. It has not been as successful as originally anticipated and is not highly recommended.

SELF EVALUATION QUESTIONS

1. What are two important considerations in properly fitting a bowling ball?
2. What are the three basic grips found in bowling balls?
3. How would you find the proper span for a conventional grip?

HOLDING THE BALL

In order to obtain maximum accuracy and consistency, it is absolutely essential that the hand position be held constant throughout the stance, swing and delivery. This action will assist in allowing the ball to be delivered exactly the same on each ball delivery.

The most effective ball delivery is the one which results in the ball hooking slightly from right to left towards the end of the ball roll. This delivery is called a hook ball and is highly desirable since there is a ball rotation from right to left (right-handers) which allows the ball to enter the pins at a slight angle minimizing deflection and maximizing "digging" action. (Figure 3.4). This entire action, in turn, results in maximum pin carry by splattering the pins more sideways as the ball continues to roll into the 5 pin in the center of the triangle. The ball

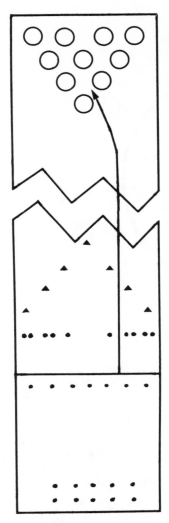

Figure 3.4 The path of a hook ball due to the fingers lifting off the center of the ball from the 4 o'clock position. The result is a counter-clockwise rotation.

Figure 3.5 While taking the stance position, the ball is held in the non-bowling hand.

rotation imparted on the ball is merely an automatic result of the fingers applying pressure on the ball from the 4 o'clock position which is off the center of the ball.

In finding the correct hand position for the hook ball, visualize the ball with a clock face on it. The center of the clock face is between the finger and thumb holes of the ball. Standing in the appropriate

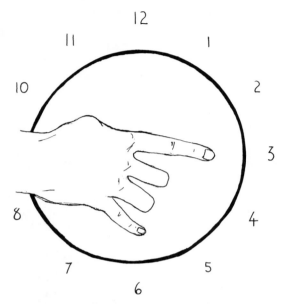

Figure 3.6 The 10-4 o'clock hand position used to deliver a hook ball.

position with the ball supported in the non-bowling hand, (Figure 3.5) the bowler places the thumb and finger holes in a 10 and 4 o'clock position, respectively. (Figure 3.6)

By turning the ball face now slightly to the right but maintaining the 10 and 4 concept, the fingers and thumb are inserted and the wrist will be found firm and straight in relation to the bowler's forearm.

Good control is associated with gripping the ball firmly. Spread the two outside fingers apart and press downward against the surface of the ball with the tips of the fingers. This will help keep the wrist firm to create maximum control at delivery.

SELF EVALUATION QUESTIONS

1. Why is a hook ball recommended?
2. In what position are the thumb and fingers placed in the ball to roll a hook ball?
3. How can you firm the wrist while gripping the ball?

AIMING IN BOWLING

There are two main ways to aim in bowling—pin bowling and spot bowling. Pin bowling, used primarily by novice bowlers, is little more than sighting at the pins at the end of the lane. Spot bowling, which

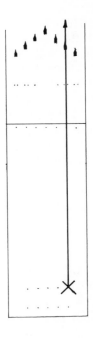

Figure 3.7 During spot bowling, the second arrow from the right becomes the prime target for right handed bowlers.

has been found to be the most successful and accurate method, is aiming at the target arrows 15 feet in front of the foul line.

Of the two, spot bowling is the preferred method of aiming due to the consistency it promotes. Consistency is very important in the game of bowling and aiming is no exception. In spot bowling for right-handed bowlers, the second and third target arrows from the right will be the constant targets. (Figure 3.7) For left-handed bowlers, it will be the second and third arrows from the left.

What are the advantages of spot bowling? First of all, it is undeniably easier to hit a target 15 feet away than one 60 feet away. Secondly, all bowling lanes are constructed the same so the bowler has a uniform place to focus the eyes and make rational adjustments. Spot bowling also creates better approach form by keeping a more balanced finishing position. Finally, it assists with the follow through motion of the release by giving the bowler something toward which to extend the delivery arm.

Pin Placement in Relation to Target Arrows

It has been previously established that the pins are setting in a perfect 36-inch triangle on the pin deck. We have also noted that the lane is made up of 39 boards with head pin centered on the 20th board. Keep in mind the pins are 12 inches apart from the center to center. Also remember that the target arrows on the lane and all of the locator dots on the approach are spaced 5 boards apart.

It should be noted that these target arrows *do not* line up with the pins, since the pins are 5 1/2 boards apart. The head pin is located on the 20th board; the 2 pin is near the 26th board; and the 3 pin is setting near the 14th board. With this in mind, one sees that the right-hander's pocket for a "perfect" strike is halfway between the head pin and 3 pin (1-3). This pocket is the 17th board. The Brooklyn pocket for right-handers is between the head pin and the 2 pin which is the 23rd board, or the 17th board for the left-handed strike ball. REMEMBER: The right side of the lane is for right-handers and they count boards and target arrows starting from the right-hand channel toward the left. The left side of the lane is for left-handers and they count boards and target arrows starting from the left-hand edge.

SELF EVALUATION QUESTIONS

1. How many boards apart are the pins?
2. Do they line up with the target arrows and locator dots?
3. On which board do we find the following:
   - a. Head pin
   - b. 2 pin
   - c. 3 pin
   - d. 1-3 pocket
   - e. 1-2 pocket for left-handers

Perfect Strike Pin Action

It is every bowler's dream to roll a perfect game of 300 which is stringing twelve strikes in a row. Such an accomplishment is elusive at best. To obtain the perfect strike in comparison to a "sloppy" or "lucky" strike, it is an absolute necessity for the ball to roll into that 1-3 pocket crossing the 17th board at an angle (Figure 3.8)

In a perfect strike, the ball only contacts four pins on its way throuth to the pit area—the 1, 3, 5 and 9 pins. The rest of the pinfall is due to a chain reaction of falling pins. If the ball's angle of entry is exact, hitting the correct impact point on the head pin, the result will be the head pin falling into the 2 pin; the 2 pin falling into the 4; and the 4 pin. This row of pins 1, 2, 4, 7 is called the "accuracy line" of pins. As a result of hitting the correct impact point on the 3 pin, it will fall in the opposite direction taking out the 6 pin with 6 pin hitting the 10 pin. This line of pins (3, 6, 10) is called the "carry line." The ball with its driving action should contact the 5 pin which in turn falls into the 8 pin. Finally, the ball itself hits the 9 pin. (Figure 3.9).

Figure 3.8 Ball hitting the 1-3 pocket.

This entire successive domino action results in a "perfect" strike. It is a result of the ball entering the pocket on the exact board, at the exact angle, with sufficient ball weight and enough roll to avoid undue ball deflection.

SELF EVALUATION QUESTIONS

1. What are the two impact points for a perfect strike?
2. In the following diagram of the pins, show the ball and pin action for a perfect strike.

STARTING POSITION

Now that we have a basic understanding of what our bowling ball is supposed to accomplish as it hits the pins, it is now time to examine possibly the most important part of bowling technique, the starting position on the approach.

NOTE: Since the 4-step approach is the easiest approach to learn and to get some semblance of timing, rhythm, and a feeling for the movement of the ball, we will be presenting everything from a 4-step basis.

In order to find a place on the approach as a point of origin or starting position, two questions must be answered: (1) How far from the foul line should the stance be taken to start the approach and (2) On which dot or board should the feet be placed in order to roll the ball over the second target arrow?

To find the distance from the foul line, a bowler should go to the foul line and turn his/her back to the pins. The heels are placed in front of

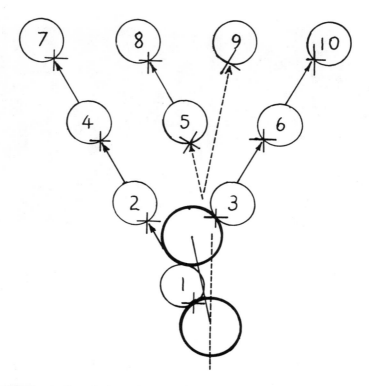

Figure 3.9 The ball and pin action in a perfect strike. (Courtesy of NBC)

the locator dots. While keeping the eyes focused on the far wall, the bowler takes either three steps and a slide or four steps plus another half step toward the end of the approach area. The spot where the last foot ended will make the correct starting distance from the line. This position may be adjusted slightly as need arises. Most bowlers of an average height and average temperament will end up around the 12 foot line.

The distance may vary from individual to individual due to (1) the length of the legs, (2) height of the individual, and (3) the type of personality (e.g. The active person will take livelier and longer steps than the slow, easy-going person).

The second assessment that must be made concerns the lateral placement of the feet on the approach. The exact board from which a bowler should start is, again, somewhat individualistic because it depends upon the shoulder and hip width of the individual. The best measurement a bowler has is to stand far enough left on the

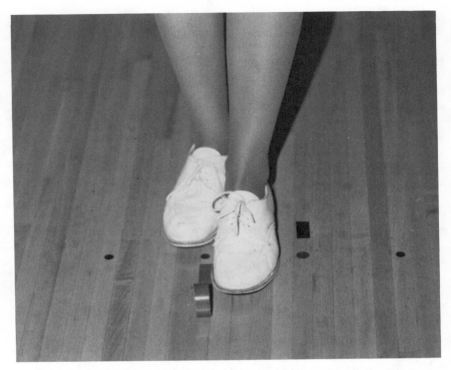

Figure 3.10 Checking the exact location of the inside edge of the left foot in the stance position.

approach so the right arm, hanging at the side, is in direct line with the target arrow, or in other words, with the locator dots corresponding to the 10th board.

Looking down at the inside edge of the left shoe (right-hander's), note the exact location of the inside edge of that foot. This will be your starting position and should remain constant in order for you to gain accuracy and consistency. (Figure 3.10).

SELF EVALUATION QUESTIONS

1. How far back on the approach should you stand?
2. How do you measure this?
3. How do you know where your left foot should be placed in your stance?
4. How many steps are recommended for the approach?

For left-handers, everything would be just the opposite. The left arm must be in line with the second arrow from the left. The right foot is the foot used to find the correct point of origin of the stance, since it is the foot on which the slide is taken at the end of the approach.

In Preparing for Action We Have Now Found:

- The bowling ball should be the proper weight and fit.
- Right-handed bowlers should wear right-handed shoes and vice versa for left-handed bowlers.
- In order for a perfect strike to occur, the ball must enter the 1-3 pocket at an angle and be equidistant between the 1 and 3 pin (1 and 2 for left-handers).
- The pins are spaced approximately 5 1/2 boards apart so the 1-3 pocket is halfway between each of the pins or three boards to the right of the head pin, 17th board.
- In order to roll a hook ball, the ball is held with the thumb at the 10 o'clock position and the fingers at 4'oclock.
- There are two main methods of aiming—pin bowling and spot bowling—but the most accurate and easiest to learn of the two is spot bowling.
- In spot bowling, the second and third target arrows from the right, found approximately 15 feet in front of the foul line, are the point of aim for right-handed bowlers. The second and third target arrows from the left are the targets for left-handed bowlers.
- The ball only strikes four pins in a perfect strike. The remaining pins are a result of pin action and deflection.
- Proper foot placement for the stance point of origin is twofold; (1) distance from the foul line and (2) lateral placement to line up the bowling arm with the second target arrow.

TEACHING CUES

Ball Selection:

- While supporting the ball, have the bowler place a pencil under the palm of the hand. If the finger span is correct, this pencil will not slide out easily.
- Place the ball on a solid surface. Insert the thumb and fingers. If it is a proper fit, the little finger can be tucked under the palm.

Hand Position and the Hook Ball:

- Visualize shaking hands with the target arrow.
- Visualize gripping a suitcase with the thumb to the left.
- In order to check for a straight wrist, have the student observe his/her own wrist. There whould not be any wrinkles.

Spot Bowling:

Instructor could go out and point to, or place a foot, on the correct arrow. When the bowler starts the release, remove the finger or foot.

Point of Origin:

While taking steps back from the foul line to find the proper distance from the foul line to start the approach, make sure the bowler keeps his/her eyes forward above the settee area or on the far wall. These steps should be taken and measured off briskly.

Correct Foot Placement:

- In a one-on-one situation, the instructor or partner should stand at the foul line facing the student and make sure the bowler's fingertips are dangling over the locator dots in line with the 10th board.
- The student could place the ball on the corresponding 10th board and position himself/herself in a lowered position beside the ball so as he/she reaches down, the fingers will dangle through the middle of the ball.

4

Stance, Approach, and Delivery Concepts

Since most of the errors in bowling are directly related to the approach, it is imperative that a basic approach model be developed which utilizes concepts applicable to everyone. Of the millions of bowlers in the world, no two bowlers bowl exactly the same. This is due to many variables such as the difference in personalities, body structure, strength, and motivation. Sometimes it is very difficult to distinguish between a person's style and those principles and concepts which are common to all good bowlers.

There are at least four fundamental concepts that apply to all bowlers—good flexibility, balance, timing, and direction. All bowlers need to incorporate these concepts into their game through the practice of efficient movement principles. In this developmental process, the goal should be the fluid integration of the mechanical principles while acquiring a natural feeling for the rhythm of the approach and delivery.

FLEXIBILITY AND STANCE

Once the point of origin for the approach has been established, it is important that the body assume a flexible position before starting the approach. This flexibility in the beginning will follow the bowler throughout the entire delivery and once lost, cannot be retrieved.

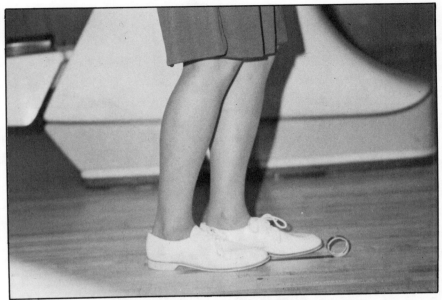

Figure 4.1 The placement of the toe of the right foot opposite the instep of the left foot.

Flexibility is insured by making several conscious body adjustments in the stance position. To prepare for a 4-step approach, the bowler should place the left foot slightly forward of the right so the toe of the right foot is somewhere near the instep of the left foot. The feet are parallel, and about two inches apart. (Figure 4.1). The mass of the body weight should be shifted to the ball of the left foot. These two actions will result in a bowler automatically stepping out with the right foot, eliminating the worry of which foot steps first.

The most important ingredient in our flexibility concept is the establishment of a small degree of flexion in the knees. It is this knee flexion that allows all other things to happen correctly. To maintain good body balance, the bowler should lean forward slightly from the hips, keeping the back relatively straight.

BALANCE AND THE STANCE

Good balance is a very important aspect of bowling. The vertical balance line can be found in an upright body simply by drawing an imaginary straight line from the shoulders through the knees perpendicular to the floor. The more the knees bend, the more the shoulders have to tilt forward in order for the body to remain in balance. When a bowler is balanced, he/she will feel comfortable. (Figure 4-2).

Figure 4.2 The vertical balance line in the stance.

Figure 4.3 Holding the ball off to the right of the body in the stance.

Figure 4.4 Side view of the ball held to the right in the stance showing the forearm resting on the hip.

Figure 4.5 The ball can be held shoulder high.

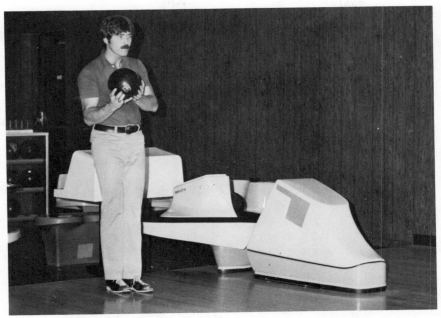

Figure 4.6 In the stance, the bowler should maintain a balanced and flexible position.

The ball should be supported in the non-bowling hand until the point of origin on the approach is reached. When ready to assume the stance poisition, the fingers should be inserted into the ball first. Next the thumb is inserted all the way down to the webbing. With the thumb and fingers at the 10 and 4 o'clock position, it is recommended that the right-handed bowler hold the ball toward the right side of the body, approximately at waist level with the right forearm resting on the hip. (Figure 4.3, 4.4). Many problems will stem from a ball held in the center of the body primarily because the ball must be swung out and around the clear the hips. This would result in an inconsistent round-house swing, a swing that goes out and away from the body. Since it is important to keep everything in a straight line, holding the ball to the right locates it properly for the pendular swing pattern.

If the ball does not feel comfortable at waist height, it may be adjusted anywhere between the waist and shoulder as long as it remains to the right of the body. (Figure 4.5). If held at shoulder height, the elbows would be resting on the hips. In this position, the ball is found near the balance line regardless of whether it is waist or shoulder high. When balanced, the ball will not feel as heavy as it would if held in front of the bowler outside the balance line. Again, it should feel comfortable. We are well on the way to a good approach when we have established a balanced stance position with a degree of flexibility. (Figure 4.6).

SELF EVALUATION QUESTIONS
1. What are the ingredients of a good stance?
2. How can flexibility be introduced into the stance?

TIMING AND PUSHAWAY

The most important part of the bowling approach is the pushaway. It creates timing for the entire approach, swing and delivery. The pushaway is the movement of the ball away from the body which sets the approach and the swing in motion.

The key feature of this concept is that the ball initates all movement. The ball is moved approximately three inches outward and downward to a point where the elbow straightens. The left hand leaves the ball at the end of the pushaway movement. At this point the balance line of the stance has been intentionally destroyed. Since an unbalanced position has been assumed, the bowler will tilt further forward and react by taking a step in order to keep the body from falling forward. (Figures 4.7, 4.8, 4.9). This cause and effect motion will always happen at the same identical point, consistently and automatically.

Figure 4.7 The pushaway initiates all movement in the approach.

Figure 4.8 The first step in the approach on the right foot is the consequence of the forward motion initiated by the pushaway.

Figure 4.9 The downward direction of the pushaway showing the straightening of the elbow.

Figure 4.10 The point to best check for proper swing and approach co-ordination is on the second step. The ball should just start into the backswing.

The length of the first step is in direct relationship to the length of the pushaway. The farther out the ball is pushed, the longer the first step will be.

To check for proper timing of the swing in relation to the steps, the second step should be observed. On the second step, the ball should be just starting upward into the backswing. (Figure 4.10)

REMEMBER: Move the ball out and in a downward direction and let the feet follow the natural urge to put the body into motion.

FLEXIBILITY AND BALANCE IN THE APPROACH

The flexibility and balance obtained in the stance should follow throughout the entire approach. In order to maintain the vertical balance line in the approach, flex the knees and take shuffling steps on the balls of the feet instead of using walking steps with a heel-toe action. A shuffle is merely a graceful gliding or skating motion across the surface of the approach. This gliding action prevents the body from bouncing up and down and breaking the rhythm of the approach and swing.

The 4-step approach is really three shuffles and a slide. With each shuffle the knees progressively increase their flexion allowing the body and the ball to be progressively lowered toward the floor for a smooth delivery. (Figure 4.11)

Figure 4.11 Showing the increased knee flexion during the approach.

DIRECTION IN THE APPROACH AND DELIVERY

The last concept in the approach model is direction. This concept includes achieving direction towards the target, accuracy in terms of the release, a complete follow-through and finishing position.

A good swing will have the following ingredients resulting in the needed accuracy:

- The ball should swing through a natural pendular arc at its own rate of speed. The speed of the swing is directly related to the length of the arm and the weight of the ball.
- The height of the arc in the backswing should equal the height of the pushaway.
- The arm should follow the natural swing of the ball. The bowler adjusts the rate of the steps to the swing rather than intentionally tampering with the pendular swing in order to match the feet.
- The pendular swing should remain in a straight line with the elbow "grazing" the hip as its moves back and forth.

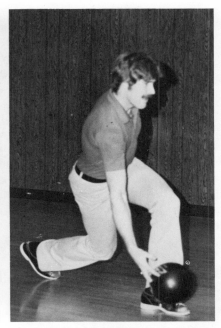

Figure 4.12 The 10-4 o'clock position should be held throughout the swing and delivery.

Figure 4.13 The thumb releases from the ball before the fingers.

- On the downswing going into the release, a slight acceleration often occurs providing extra impetus to the "lift" and rotation mechanism at the point of release.

For the beginning bowler the release is very simple. The 10-4 o'clock position that was established in the stance is maintained throughout the swing and is still present in the finishing position. (Figure 4.12) The wrist remains firm and straight and the forearm rotates minimally in the swing and release. The sliding foot should point toward the target.

As the ball is released on the far side of the foul line, the thumb should come out of the ball before the fingers (Figure 4.13), allowing the lifting action of the fingers in the 4 o'clock position to occur as the ball starts upward in the pendular swing. (Figure 4.14) This creates a force off the center of the ball which results in a right to left rotation of the ball. The resultant ball roll will find the ball going straight approximately two-thirds of the way down the lane and then, due to the frictional forces equalizing, the ball will start hooking from right to left. This action allows the ball to be rolled over the second arrow (10th board) and hook into the 1-3 pocket (17th board) at the proper angle.

The last factor that assists in achieving good direction is the follow through. A good follow through will find the bowler's eyes still focusing on the target and the straightened bowling arm moving forward in direct line with the target arrow. (Figure 4.15)

SELF EVALUATION QUESTIONS

1. What initiates the forward motion of the body?
2. Where is the ball moved in the pushaway phase?
3. With each shuffle what happens to the knees?
4. In what position are the thumb and fingers held throughout the swing and delivery?
5. What happens at the delivery with the thumb? The fingers?
6. On which target arrow should the ball roll?

VERTICAL BALANCE LINE AND THE DELIVERY

Throughout the stance and the approach, the shoulders are kept over flexed knees for the maintenance of good balance. This vertical balance line already established is also very important in a bowler's finishing position to allow a smooth and consistent delivery. By bending the knees rather than the bending at the waist or dropping the

Figure 4.14 The "lift" placed on the ball as it is released while the arm continues upward into the pendular swing.

Figure 4.15 The follow-through.

Figure 4.16 Increased knee flexion lowers the body to the necessary delivery level.

Figure 4.17 The vertical balance line is maintained throughout the delivery and follow-through.

shoulders, the bowler can get closer to the floor which aids in placing the ball on the lane rather than dropping it. (Figure 4.16) After a well-balanced delivery the body can maintain a comfortable follow through position. (Figure 4.17)

HORIZONTAL BALANCE LINE
AND THE FINISH POSITION

Besides the vertical balance line, there is also a proper horizontal balance line which is critical in the finish position. In order to counterbalance the weight of the bowling ball which is moving in front and to the side of the body, the body must make other adjustments. The opposite arm becomes a counterbalance by being stretched out and angles a little backwards. This procedure assists in keeping the shoulders and hips square to the target. (Figure 4.18)

The most crucial adjustment for horizontal balance at the delivery is accomplished for right-handed bowlers by stretching the right leg backwards in a straightened position and letting it drift to the left in a pigeon-toed position. by turning the toe inward in this pigeon-toed position, the hip curls under, opening the right side. This allows the

Figure 4.18 Counterbalancing the weight of the ball by extending the opposite arm. (Horizontal balance)

Figure 4.19 The complete delivery and follow-through form with the ball going over the second arrow.

ball to swing in an unobstructed straight line toward the target. Caution should be taken here because if the leg is kicked around behind, it will jerk the torso out of alignment. To prevent this from happening, the bowler should try to keep the toe on the approach and let it slide into place.

HAND AND ARM POSITION IN THE FOLLOW THROUGH

After the ball has been delivered, the bowling arm continues to move forward in a direct line with the target arrow. The finish position should find a 90 degree angle formed between the shoulder, the arm, and the target with the fingers curled into the palm of the hand. The eyes remain focused on the target arrow and should be able to identify the exact board over which the ball is rolled. (Figure 4.19)

SELF EVALUATION QUESTIONS

1. How is the body lowered in order to lay the ball on the floor in the delivery?
2. What body adjustment must be made to counterbalance the weight of the ball in the approach? The delivery?
3. Explain the action of the trailing leg in the delivery.
4. Explain the finish position of the arms and fingers.

SUMMARY OF BOWLING FUNDAMENTALS
(For Right-Hand Bowlers)

Stance
- The left foot is placed slightly forward of the right with the majority of the body weight on the ball of the left foot.
- The knees are unlocked and slightly flexed. The shoulders are tilted forward slightly from the hips and directly above the knees.
- The ball is supported in the non-bowling hand until the point of origin is found and the stance has been assumed.
- The thumb and fingers of the bowling hand are now inserted into ball at the 10 and 4 o'clock position, fingers first.
- The ball is held to the right front of the body at approximately waist height with the forearm resting on the hip. The ball is near the vertical balance line drawing through the shoulders and knees and is supported slightly by the non-bowling hand.
- The shoulders and hips should be square to the intended line of ball roll.

Pushaway
- The most crucial part of the approach and swing is in timing the pushaway with the approach.
- The pushaway is a movement of the ball out from the body in a downward direction resulting in the straightening of the bowling arm.
- The pushaway action puts the body in an unbalanced position and will cause the body to take a step forward.
- The step forward will be with the right foot which was the unweighted back foot in the stance.

Approach
- During the approach, the feet will take three shuffle steps and a slide.
- Each shuffle step will find the knees progressively more flexed.
- The shuffle should be in a straight line moving towards the target arrow.
- The eyes of the bowler are focused solely on the target.
- If the swing and the approach are coordinated, the ball will be just starting to move upward into the backswing on the second step.

Swing

- The weight of the ball straightens the elbow on the pushaway which is the start of the arc for the pendular swing.
- The ball swings straight back in the natural pendular swing to the height of the backswing, somewhere between the waist and the shoulder.
- During this swing the 10-4 o'clock thumb-finger position is maintained with a firm forearm and extended wrist.
- The wrist remains firm throughout the swing, including the peak backswing position.
- The shoulders and hips are square to the target throughout the swing.
- The non-bowling arm is extended to the side and slightly back for balance.

Delivery

- The slide is accomplished by bending the knees to the point where the ball can swing out on the lane without being dropped or dropping the shoulder.
- The shoulders are moved forward from the hips and aligned directly over the knees in order to keep the vertical balance line intact.
- In order to counterbalance the weight of the ball that has moved in front of the vertical balance line, the right leg is extended back and drifts to the left in a pigeon-toed fashion.
- The hips and shoulders remain square to the target.
- The ball is released on the far side of the foul line as it starts upward in the pendular swing.
- On the release, the thumb and fingers are still in the 10-4 o'clock position.
- The thumb is automatically released from the ball first and then the fingers with an upward lifting action. The off-center lift will cause the ball to have a right to left (counterclockwise) rotation, resulting in a slight hook.

Follow Through

- The eyes remain focused on the target arrow.
- The bowling arm moves forward in a direct line with the target arrow.
- The fingers are curled toward the palm of the hand.
- The finish position is a 90 degree angle formed between the shoulder, the arm, and the target.

TEACHING CUES

Pushaway

- To teach the correct length, direction, or height of the pushaway, the instructor can hold a finger or hand at the estimated length of the pushaway by standing sideways on the approach. This is also useful for pushaways that are excessively high or low.
- To teach the proper arc of the pushaway and the proper ball-foot coordination, crouch in front of the student facing him/her and have the student push the ball into your hands. This action should be followed by the first step in the approach.

Approach

- To practice shuffling without the ball, have the student try keeping his/her footwork quiet and noiseless. The noise should resemble sandpaper rubbing across wood. Emphasize that shuffling is achieved without decreasing the flexion of the knees.
- To keep the student from bouncing during the approach, have the student visualize taking the approach with a glass of water on each shoulder.
- To eliminate "drifting" and "wandering," have student visualize taking the approach on a gymnastic balance beam.
- To eliminate "drifting," place a towel or piece of paper on the approach near the foul line and have the bowler slide to the side of it.
- To show correct direction of the pushaway and swing, proper coordination of step and swing, and firmness of the wrist, the instructor could stand to the bowler's side. Using the left hand to hold the student's right wrist, move the bowler through the entire approach and swing.
- To coordinate the armswing and the footwork into a smooth, rhythmical approach, use the cadence: "Push-swing-and-roll." The student should take a step with every word. The instructor can accentuate the word desired.

Arm Swing

- To emphasize the natural pendular motion of the arm swing, have the student visualize the arm as the pendulum of a large clock. Take practice swings, allowing the ball to swing in the natural pendular motion and rate of speed.
- To emphasize the shoulder stability in the swing, place your fingers on the student's shoulder while practice swings are taken. The fingers should remain stationary.

- To assist in keeping the swing straight, emphasize the elbow grazing past the hip.

Ball Release

- To practice mechanics of the release, have the bowler use one step only while close to the foul line.
- To emphasize the finger gripping, have the students practice gripping the ball with the finger with the pressure on the tips of the gripping fingers. The thumb shold release at the ankle.
- To practice the release point beyond the foot and foul line, place a towel, 6 to 10 inches wide, on the lane on the other side of the foul line. Have the student release the ball on the far side of the towel.
- To assist in teaching "lift," have the student visualize squeezing a gun trigger as the ball comes off the hand in the release. The instructor could also have the student feel the fingertip pressure in the ball and upon the release, curl the fingers into the palm of the hand.

Body Balance in the Release and Follow Through

- To assist in staying low and in balance throughout the release and follow through, have the bowler at release point visualize extending the knee cap over the foul line (not the head).
- To establish proper vertical and horizontal balance lines without a ball, have the bowler imitate the finish position:
  1. Extend the sliding foot forward.
  2. Shift all of the body weight to the sliding foot.
  3. Bend the knee.
  4. Extend the trailing leg far back until the knee straightens.
  5. Place the trailing leg so it is stretched out behind the forward ankle.
  6. Slightly pigeon-toe the trailing foot while keeping it in contact with the floor. Have them "freeze" in this position after each delivery of the ball until the ball passes the target.
- To assist in keeping the right foot in contact with the floor as it slides into the trailing leg position, have the bowler pretend there is gum on the little toe of that shoe.
- To insure the proper use of the balance arm and avoid a "dropped shoulder," visualize holding a bucket of water with the left hand. This can also be stressed by having the student stretch the left arm as far as possible away from the body.

Follow Through

- To emphasize the arm position on the follow-through, have the student "freeze" the arm so it is directly in front of the right shoulder with the arm extending toward the target.
- To correct an insufficient follow-through or an incorrect direction, have the student visualize holding a glass of water in the bowling hand. At the release point, visualize tossing the water up and over the shoulder, keeping the elbow straight as long as possible.

5

Principles of Movement Applied to Bowling

As was previously noted, it is important to know the "whys and where-fores" when learning or trying to improve a skill. By knowing the concepts and principles involved in effective movement, learning can be enhanced by making it more meaningful. Analysis and error correction then becomes second nature.

We are possibly all familiar with Newton's Law of Motion that states, "An object which is at rest or is in motion will remain at rest or in motion at the same speed, in a straight line, unless acted upon by an outside force." This principle will be our chief guide throughout our bowling swing, approach, and delivery. In order to analyze each phase of this physical law, many other concepts and principles enter the picture.

WEIGHT OF THE BALL

It has been previously noted that weight is an important consideration when selecting a ball. Each bowler should select a ball that is as heavy as he/she can control. The reason for this is quite obvious when one considers the principle of force and gravity. In an underarm swing pattern, gravity will cause the ball to swing in a straight, pendular fashion unless restricted or acted upon by another force. If the ball is heavy enough, and if a bowler will allow this natural swing, force will

Figure 5.1 The ball can be held high in the stance for the production of more momentum.

be produced by gravity and momentum, not by the bowler "muscling" and forcing the ball. In this natural swing pattern, the direction of the swing will always remain constant, and if lined up correctly, will remain in a straight line. If the ball is too light, a bowler has the tendency to push or pull the ball off his natural swing line resulting in inconsistency. Additionally, the heavier ball will usually result in greater pin fall. This is because the heavier ball does not deflect as easily as the lighter ball when it contacts the weight of the pins.

FORCE PRODUCTION

It is essential that enough force be generated at delivery to allow the ball to travel effectively on course. Force is generated during the swing and the approach.

Swing

The production of gravital force in the swing is directly related to the following principle. The greater distance the swinging object travels, the more time for gravity to act on the ball, thereby producing more force. Consequently, a ball held higher in the stance, all things being equal, would result in a longer arc because the backswing would equal the height of the pushaway. (Figure 5.1) The ball would be traveling a greater distance thus allowing gravity to have more time to act on the ball, resulting in more ball velocity at the time of delivery.

A bowler having trouble producing enough force at the delivery may want to try holding the ball higher in the stance. Gradual changes are recommended to maintain good form and consistency.

Another way of allowing the ball to travel a greater distance in the swing is to lengthen the lever that is moving through space. That lever, the bowler's arm, should be completely straightened in the pushaway and the backswing to allow for maximum length.

Because of the added weight of the ball and the momentum that the ball is gathering, the body must remain stable and firm throughout the entire swing. By stabilizing the shoulder and wrist of the swinging arm, the pendular swing will stay in a straight line. This stabilizing action will also keep the shoulder from dropping and free it from muscle strain. Stabilizing the wrist during all phases of the swing, particularly the backswing, merely keeps the ball from straying off the desired pendular path.

Approach

The main purpose of an approach is to gather forward body momentum that will be transferred to the ball at the release. Since a gravital swing alone will not build up enough momentum to roll the ball at a speed great enough to hold the desired line and successfully knock down the pins, it is necesssary to add an approach to assist in this force production.

The principle of time and distance becomes important when developing momentum in the approach. The greater the time and distance over which momentum is developed, the greater the force imparted. Therefore, the longer and faster the approach, all things being equal, the greater the momentum build-up. Many times this results in bowlers running to the foul line from the end of the approach so the ball will have greater momentum. Erroneously, they assume that this fast ball will scare the pins down. Remember, in bowling everything is controlled and coordinated. An approach should only be as long and as fast as needed to coordinate with the swing, to hold the desired line to the pins, and to knock the pins down.

Here are some factors to keep in mind while developing momentum in the approach.

- Shuffle steps will allow for a smoother approach. By keeping the body free from bounding, all energies will be directed to building forward momentum. Outside forces acting on the ball swing will be kept to a minimum and the ball will remain in its natural arc.

- The vertical balance line should be shifted forward throughout the approach. The forward shift of body weight should be from the ankles. This helps in many ways:
  1. It will place the center of gravity in front of the pushing foot for ease in building momentum during the steps.
  2. It will assure a smooth approach by allowing the knees to act as shock absorbers in each step.
  3. It will increase the arc of the ball due to the body leaning slightly forward, allowing for greater force production.
  4. It assures the body a position over a bent knee upon release for a smooth, straight delivery.
  5. It forces the point of maximum momentum to coincide with the ball delivery over the foul line.
  6. It allows the arm swing to continue forward for a greater distance in the follow through for maximum momentum and direction.

It is almost impossible for a bowler who is standing erect or approaching in an erect fashion to shift his/her weight forward upon the delivery of the ball. In this erect position, the body's center of gravity is high and the body weight is slightly back. As a result, the ball will be released beside or behind the left foot with the swing going in an upward direction and the ball crossing the lane.

If the forward weight shift comes from the waist rather than the ankles, the hips will remain high, resulting in an unbalanced body during approach and delivery, with the majority of the force production going downward into the floor rather than out onto the lane. The resultant follow through will be incomplete with very little chance for "lift" to be placed on the ball.

- At all times during the approach, the toes, feet and body should be going in a straight line for maximum mechanical efficiency. This allows the feet to push directly from behind and also allows for all momentum to be directed and released in the direction of the target.

How much momentum or ball speed is really needed to get an effective ball roll? It should be noted that all good bowlers develop a specific optimal ball speed. Research has determined optimal ball speed at delivery of 17 miles per hour or 2.4 seconds from point of release to the head pin. At this speed, all governing forces will be in proper balance allowing the ball to hit pins with the most effective impact. This speed allows the pins to topple in a domino fashion rather than flying straight up as with a fast ball. A slower ball will deflect as it hits the pins causing ineffective pin action.

HOOK BALL AND MOMENTUM

After first released, the ball is traveling at the maximum speed, and slides more than rolls in a straight line. This is due partly to the speed of the ball of the lane. Frictional forces build up between the ball and the lane and slow the ball. As the ball slows, the side rotation imparted by the fingers lifting the ball off the center of gravity (4 o'clock position) now takes effect. When this side rotation becomes greater than the forward roll, the ball begins to hook towards the pocket.

When the ball speed, forward roll, and side rotation forces are in proper balance, the result will be an effective, consistent, working hook ball.

CORRECTION SUGGESTIONS
FOR CHANGING BALL SPEEDS

Any time changes are to be made in the speed of the ball, it is of great importance to maintain good coordination, flexibility, balance and timing of the swing and approach.

Not Enough Ball Speed

When a bowler is having trouble generating enough speed on the ball, it will hook too far to the left. This is due to too little slide and too much side rotation. Any of five different corrections may resolve the problem.

- The ball may be held higher in the stance which will automatically create a longer arc.
- The ball may be pushed away a bit farther on the pushaway.
- A 5-step approach may be used to give a longer approach to produce more forward momentum. If a 5-step approach is used, the ball is held higher and pushed out a little farther in order for the swing to be properly coordinated.
- The approach may be started at least 6 inches further back.
- A lighter ball could be used.

Too Much Ball Speed

Some rethinking may be in order for those who are intent on throwing the ball as hard as they can. They are probably leaving pocket splits, often the 5 pin, and not getting effective pin action. These bowlers will continue to do so unless their mental attitude is changed by someone who can prove why that type of ball is not the most effective. A fast ball results in too much slide and not enough side rotation so the hook is very minimal. The following suggestions could be used.

Figure 5.2 Keeping the shoulders and hips square to the target results in more accuracy.

- In the stance, holding the ball lower to decrease the resistance of the swing.
- The pushaway could be shortened or de-emphasized.
- The knees can be flexed more because it is very difficult for anyone to move fast with flexed knees.
- Use the force of gravity to move the ball in the swing rather than forcing the ball. Flex the knees more, pushing the ball out lower, and not quite so far. This should allow the bowler to feel the natural weight of the ball swinging the arm rather than his/her arm doing the swinging. He/she should constantly feel relaxed.
- The approach could be started at least 6 inches closer.
- A heavier ball could be used.

ACCURACY AND CONSISTENCY PRINCIPLES

Once force production is present, a bowler must move his force in a consistent movement pattern in order to insure accuracy. To establish accuracy and consistency in the swing, approach and delivery, everything must move in straight lines toward the designated target.

The swing must stay in a straight forward and backward arc. Holding the ball off to the right side while in the stance will assure that it will travel in this straight instead of moving in a circular pattern around the hips. Stabilizing the shoulders and wrist in the swing will also assist in keeping the swing straight.

The approach must be in a fairly straight line while moving toward the designated target. The shoulders and hips should be perpendicular to this target line as the feet move in a straight line toward the target. By keeping the upper body position square to the target, the swing will also stay square to the target. (Figure 5.2)

The 10 o'clock position must remain constant throughout the swing. In order to maintain this position, the wrist must remain firm and the forearm must not rotate.

Upon the release of the ball, everything is still square to the intended line of aim, the shoulders, the hips, the swing, and the follow through. In order to fulfill and control the square to square concept, the entire body must be in perfect balance. (Figure 5.3)

Controlling the entire body in the approach and the swing will insure the bowler of rolling the ball the same way time after time. Once this consistency is conquered, the bowler can now start making accurate adjustments.

Figure 5.3 Upon delivery, the entire body is square to the target.

In summary, looking back upon Newton's Law of Motion that states an object which is at rest or in motion will remain at rest or in motion at the same speed, in a straight line, unless acted upon by an outside force, we find that every part of this law applies to bowling force production and accuracy. It is every bowler's objective to control the variables in the skill of bowling in order to reach his/her potential. Once these variables are identified, error correction is also very easy.

REFERENCES
Broer, Marion R. *Efficiency of Human Movement*. 2nd ed. Philadelphia, Saunders, 1966.
Culver, Elizabeth J. "Bowling." In Ainsworth, Dorothy S.: *Individual Sports for Women*, 4th ed. Philadelphia, Saunders, 1964.

6

Common Errors and Corrective Actions

The following chart of common bowling errors, effects, and corrective actions will assist a bowler or an instructor in developing diagnostic skills. However, due to the great number of movement variables and interrelationship of these movements, it is impossible to cover every possible error and give the correct diagnosis for that particular individual's error.

This chart is intended to assist the instructor in experiencing and sharpening diagnostic skills by analyzing the most common errors found in bowling. The concept of the error and corrections can more easily be identified by the cause and effect relationship as stated in the charts.

GENERAL:

ERROR	CAUSE	EFFECT	CORRECTION
Lack of pin action	Lack of lift Lack of hook Lack of ball revolutions Ball rolls over thumb hole Lofting ball Overreaching Ball too light Late release Thumb hole too tight Improper top, finger or side weight Improper pitches Ball line too far inside Ball line too far outside Skidding Ball	Pins are left standing	Note: Check all corrections for these causes. Angle and proper revolutions are key to good pin action.
Back-up ball (reverse hook) if not desired	Lack of knowledge of ball release and types of roll Thumb position at 12 o'clock and hand rotation Fingers in 6-7 o'clock position Starting with straight ball when learning to bowl Flexed wrist in stance or release Holding the ball in the middle of body Dropping right shoulder	Maximum ball deflection Lack of lift due to hyper-extended wrist rotation Lack of consistency	Correct starting position (lining up shoulder with arrow). Hold ball in 8 or 9 o'clock position in stance. Firm wrist by pressing down with 2 outside fingers. Hold ball with forearm resting on hip in stance. Flex knees.

STANCE:

ERROR	CAUSE	EFFECT	CORRECTION
Feet too far apart	Attempt at body balance	Drifting Waddling	Move feet closer together.
Improper distribution of weight	Attempt at body balance	Not starting automatically with proper foot	Place most of weight on balance-side foot
Stiff Knees	Bending too much at waist or leaning too far back	Large, awkward steps or not shuffling	Flex both knees equally.
Excessive forward body angle	Bending too much at waist	Stiff knees Loss of Balance Tendency to rush	Straighten body enough to restore correct balance line.
Ball held too high	Ball held too high trying to get speed Slight aiming over ball	Release balance hand too soon Pushaway too long Steps too long Excessive approach speed High backswing	Establish ball height which will give smooth, controlled pendulum swing and desired speed necessary.
Ball held too low	Excessive bending at waist	Push directly away too much Carrying ball during first step Timing off — body ahead of ball disrupts pendulum swing	Raise ball to desired height.

ERROR	CAUSE	EFFECT	CORRECTION
Ball held in center of body	Ball feels comfortable equally supported with both hands	Tendency to hold thumb at 12 o'clock Tendency to flex wrist Tendency to develop outside-in arm swing or wrap around swing	Move ball position in line with right shoulders.
Elbow not tucked in	Elbow not tucked in to hip in stance Holding ball in center of body	Outside-in or wrap around swing Incorrect and changing thumb position in swing	Place forearm on hipbone.
Wrist bent (Gooseneck)	Not enough pressure with index and little finger Loose grip	Ball slides too much and deflects Inconsistent delivery	Press firmly against ball with two outside fingers or give support to wrist.
Wrist cupped	Overly firm wrist muscle flex	Locked elbow and shoulder, prohibiting natural pendulum swing and release Inconsistent delivery Restricted backswing	Relax arm and let ball drop naturally.
Improper spread of outside fingers	Outside fingers either spread or close to middle fingers Lack of understanding of effects of spread of either or both index or little finger	Not achieving maximum hooking/hitting potential	Hold outside fingers close if little or no turn desired. Spread index finger for semi-roller, if extra turn desired. Spread little finger for full-roller, if extra turn desired.

ERROR	CAUSE	EFFECT	CORRECTION
Weak grip	Not enough pressure exerted with two middle fingers Not enough pressure with two outside fingers	Too much fluctuation of hand during swing Dropped ball Lack of backswing	Put tension in wrist and fingers.
Lack of concentration	Lack of confidence Distraction on approach Wandering mind Eyes not focused on target Self-induced pressure	Imperfect execution of delivery Carry-over frustration Low scores Inconsistent approach method	Develop simple, relaxed concentration—not grim, lip biting, teeth gritting determination.
Lack of relaxation	Grim determination Giving in to pressure of occasion Gripping ball too tightly Lack of proper breathing	Ball steered, pushed or pulled in delivery Inability to sustain string of strikes	Take a deep breath—exhale. Flex knees. Loosen grip slightly Feel looseness in elbow. Lean forward slightly ready for smooth pushaway step.
PUSHAWAY: Ball pushed too high	Attempt to develop speed Ball pushed up more than out Weight is back	Abrupt lowering of ball Low or high backswing Jerky swing Dropped shoulder	Push ball in a downward direction.
Ball lowered too soon (little or no pushaway)	Ball pushed down more than out Attempt to get ball in backswing, quickly Leaning forward in stance	Muscling the swing Ball not in appropriate position at conclusion of first step Poor timing—ball ahead of bowler	Push ball in a downward direction.

ERROR	CAUSE	EFFECT	CORRECTION
Pushaway too long	Attempt to straighten arm and extend to full length for full pendulum swing	Step too long Feeling of rushing	Push ball a moderate distance forward and downward. Delay straightening of elbow.
Ball pushed too far right or left	Try to clear the hip Lack of kinesthetic awareness	Developing inside out or outside in swing Missing target Dropping shoulder	Hold ball to side of body in front of shoulder and push ball toward target. Maintain thumb position created in stance.

DOWNSWING (SECOND STEP):

ERROR	CAUSE	EFFECT	CORRECTION
Balance hand released too late	Not taking balance hand off ball Fear of dropping ball	Carrying ball Hurried downswing Stiff approach	The balance hand should be disengaged, just as first step is completed.
Left hand released too early	Taking balance hand off ball too early	Muscling Hurried swing Dropped shoulder Timing off	The balance hand should be disengaged, just as first step is completed.
Ball carried	Balance hand not disengaged Lack of pushaway Not using force of gravity	Timing off Inconsistent ball speed	Balance hand should be disengaged. Let gravitational force act upon the ball.
Lack of counter balance	Balance arm not allowed to attain counter-balance position	Dropped shoulder	Simultaneously with downward motion of ball, extend the balance arm to side of and slightly away from body.

BACKSWING (THIRD STEP):

ERROR	CAUSE	EFFECT	CORRECTION
Backswing too high	Pushaway too high and too forceful Attempt to get speed by deliberately raising ball in backswing Shoulder and hip allowed to tilt forward and rotate	Shoulder/hip rotation Possible sideways finish on fourth step Sidearming delivery Too much speed	Control pushaway—let natural pendulum swing develop. Do not add speed in swing by "muscling." Flex knees and avoid bending at the waist.
Backswing too low	Inhibited swing Cupped wrist Muscling	Muscling Forced release Early turn	Develop free pendulum swing. Push the ball slightly higher in pushaway.
Shoulder and hip rotation	Pushaway too forceful Attempt to get speed by deliberately increasing backswing	May result in sideways finish in fourth step Sidearming delivery	Control pushaway—develop free pendulum swing. Do not add speed to swing by "muscling." Maintain consistent thumb position.
Hesitation at top of backswing	Bending too far forward Weight on toes Hunching shoulders	Inhibited fluid motion of swing Forced downswing	Restore body balance on balance line. Develop free pendulum swing.
Wrap-around swing	Ball held to right of shoulders in stance Ball pushed to right during first step	Inconsistent ball path and direction	Position ball in line with shoulder and push straight ahead.

TIMING (FOURTH STEP):

ERROR	CAUSE	EFFECT	CORRECTION
Body ahead of ball	Sliding too far Lack of synchronized movement Lack of balance line Pushaway started late	Body balance lost Hurried release Dropped ball Pushed or pulled ball Sidearming in delivery	Bring ball forward with slide. Restore balance line. Slide only as far as body balance can be maintained. Move the ball first in pushaway.
Not enough slide	Heel-toe approach Lack of balance line Picking up sliding foot Landing heel first Lack of flex in sliding knee	Abrupt stop Abrupt release Difficulty completing follow through	Shuffle during delivery. Develop balance line. Concentrate on sliding last step. Keep ball-side foot down longer before raising for balance.
Too much slide	Over-emphasis on slide Lack of balance line Right hip and shoulder remaining back Approach too fast	Right hip and shoulder remaining back Improper lift on ball Poor balance line	Maintain balance line during slide. Decrease speed of steps and flex knees.
Hop or skip steps	Straightening sliding—side knee, heel comes in contact with approach too soon. Ball at top of backswing too soon.	Erratic release Loss of balance	Restore balance line. Start pushaway later

ERROR	CAUSE	EFFECT	CORRECTION
Sliding Sideways	Approach too fast Insufficient sliding Lack of knee bend Starting approach too close to foul line	Inconsistent release Dropped ball Improper lift on ball	Decrease speed of steps and flex knees. Flex sliding knee.
Off balance sideways	Drifting on last step Lacking of counter balance Dropped shoulder	Pulling the ball off target Dropped shoulder Inconsistent release point—lofting or dropping	Restore balance line. Develop and maintain counter-balance. Slide straight. Flex sliding knee.
Off balance forward	Bending too much at waist Over-reaching Steering or guiding ball Lunging	Steering or guiding ball Lunging Lack of lift Late thumb release	Restore balance line. Extending arm only enough to complete pendulum swing. Flex knees. Hold shoulders more upright.
Fouling	Starting position too close Pushaway too long causing steps to be too long Excessive slide Weight back on delivery	Loss of pinfall on delivery	Control pushaway. If necessary move back approximately six inches at a time to re-establish point of origin. Establish balance line.
Side-arming	Ball held in middle of body Inside-out or outside-in swing Drifting to left	Inconsistent ball path Too much hook Missing target	Position ball in line with right shoulder. Control pushaway. Walk and slide straight to target.

ERROR	CAUSE	EFFECT	CORRECTION
Ball released too soon	Body too straight on release Anxious to put "stuff" on ball Muscling downward Bent too far forward Stiff knee Ball held too loosely Finishing position too high or too low Incorrect ball fit	Lack of lift Ball hooks too much or not enough hook	Maintain natural pendulum swing. Restore balance line. Keep firm grip with all fingers. Restore balance line. Snug thumb
Ball released too late	Overreaching Steering (guiding) ball Thumb hole too tight Too much pitch in thumb hole	Steering (guiding) ball Skidding Inconsistent ball path Weak ball—no hitting power	Maintain pendulum swing. Making sure thumb hole size and pitch allows free thumb release. Restore balance line.
RELEASE: Cut-off armswing (bent elbow)	Not extending arm forward Eagerness to apply lift Using forearm too much Improper fit of ball Span too long	Inconsistent ball path and direction Lofting ball	Maintain pendulum swing. Firmness of grip plus pendulum swing will produce desired lift and roll. Maintain straight elbow on follow through.

ERROR	CAUSE	EFFECT	CORRECTION
Dropped ball	Poor timing Throwing ball into approach or lane Too much weight on ball-side foot Holes too large and/or improper pitches Lack of balance line	Inconsistent ball path and direction	Synchronize movements. Restore balance line. Keep firm grip with all fingers. Hole sizes and pitches should allow ball control to be maintained until release beyond bottom of pendulum arc.
Lofted ball	Stiff sliding-side knee Hanging on to ball too long Holes too small and/or too much pitch	Inconsistent ball path	Restore balance line. Maintain pendulum swing. Flex sliding-side knee. Check holes for size and pitch especially thumb hole.
Not consistent in alignment and height of arm follow-through	Poor timing Lack of balance line Faulty release Over-reaching Exaggerated follow-through (Statue of Liberty) Forced completion of pendulum arc	Forced completion of pendulum arc Ball path and direction inconsistent	Synchronize movements. Restore balance line. Check release execution. Allow follow-through to be natural continuation of pendulum arc. Follow-through arm directly in front of shoulder.

OVERALL DELIVERY:

ERROR	CAUSE	EFFECT	CORRECTION
Too fast	Ball held too high Pushaway too forceful Pushaway too long Swing too fast Approach too long Bent too far forward	Poor timing Too much speed on ball Lack of hook Ball deflects	Position ball in stance to encourage controlled pushaway and pendulum swing. Decrease size of steps. Develop balance line.
Too slow	Standing too upright Uncertainty Carrying ball Approach too short Pushaway downward	Inconsistent release Too much hook Insufficient speed on ball	Develop pendulum swing. Let swing govern feet. Move point of origin back slightly. Push the ball out in a downward direction and accentuate the pushaway.
Steps too long	Exaggerated pushaway	Approach looks and feels awkward Lack of fluid motion	Shorten steps—synchronize with pendulum swing.
Steps too short	Carrying ball Ball not pushed forward enough Letting footwork govern swing	Letting footwork govern swing Poor timing Approach looks and feels awkward Lack of fluid motion	Develop smooth controlled pushaway. Let pushaway and pendulum swing govern feet.

ERROR	CAUSE	EFFECT	CORRECTION
Drifting	Not aligned properly with target Feeling of too far right or left at point of origin Facing target incorrectly Pushing ball outside or inside shoulder line First step a cross-over or side-step Outside-in or inside-out swing Side-arming in delivery	Develop outside-in or inside-out armswing Side-arming in delivery Push or pull ball at release	Align ball, shoulder and target. Push ball straight ahead toward target. Step forward straight ahead. Maintain pendulum swing.

BALL PATH AND DIRECTION:

ERROR	CAUSE	EFFECT	CORRECTION
Not enough hook	Too much speed Poor timing Overreaching Pushing Steering (guiding) ball Dropping ball Lofting Incorrect hand position Lack of lift Thumb hole too tight Overturn in release Skidding ball Ball too heavy	Lack of hitting power Lack of proper angle of entry into pocket Maximizing deflection	Synchronize movements. Maintain pendulum swing. Keep firm wrist and finger grip. Keep fingers at 4-5 o'clock position throughout swing (generally). Check ball for weight and balance weights.

ERROR	CAUSE	EFFECT	CORRECTION
Too much hook	Poor timing	Ball rolls too early	Synchronize movements.
	Pulling	Lack of accuracy	Maintain pendulum swing.
	Insufficient ball speed	Depending upon the	Check firmness of grip and
	Ball too light	weight of the ball—	wrist not cupped.
	Early release	too much angle or	Check ball for balance weights.
	Ball rolls too early	too much deflection	Lift through ball not acutely
	Outside fingers too far		counterclockwise
	on side of ball		
	Excessive lift and/or		
	excessive turn		
Ball generally too light in pocket	Excessive speed in delivery	Lack of striking power	Control pushaway and maintain
	Ball line too deep	Maximum deflection	pendulum swing.
	Ball line too far outside		Check starting and finishing
	Overreaching		position of slide foot to see
	Pushing-steering ball		if delivery foot steps are
	Lack of lift		straight.
	Rearing		Check thumb and finger position
	Skidding ball		at release point.
	Inside-out swing		Maintain firm grip with wrist
	Wrap-around swing		and fingers
	High backswing		Check balance line at release.
	Drifting		Check position of ball in
			stance.

ERROR

Ball generally too heavy in pocket

CAUSE

Slow ball
Ball line too deep
Ball line too far outside
Pulling ball
Rearing
Early release
Excessive lift
Outside-in swing
Wrap-around swing
Drifting

EFFECT

Excessive split and spare leaves
Acute angle of entry

CORRECTION

Check starting and finishing position of slide foot to see if delivery foot steps are straight.
Control pushaway and maintain pendulum swing.
Check thumb and finger position at release point.
Maintain firm grip with wrist and fingers.
Checking balance line at release.
Check position of ball in stance.
Follow through in line with shoulder.
Avoid rearing up.
Check the arm position in stance and direction of pushaway.

7

3-1-2 Strike Adjustment System

One of the more challenging aspects of the bowling game is adjusting to changing lane conditions. Even lanes within the same establishment play differently due to atmospheric conditions, time of day, the quality and amount of play, or the difference in maintenance procedures. Because of these differences in characteristics, the bowling ball may hook more or less from one lane to another. It is the bowler's responsibility to adjust to the lane. As long as the bowler can reasonably deliver the ball consistently in the same way, adjustments can be made.

The 3-1-2 strike adjustment system is based on a mathematical computation which will aid in determining how much delivery adjustment is needed. It takes the guesswork out of adjusting the strike ball delivery, but it only applies to the first delivery of a frame.

The adjustment takes place in the delivery stance after judging where the ball is consistently contacting the pins in relation to the head pin. Remember, the second target arrow remains the constant point of aim. The only thing that should be adjusted is the foot position in a new point of origin. The basic rule of thumb is to move in the direction of the error or mistake. If you deliver the ball and the ball hooks too much traveling left of the 17th board, move the stance left. If the ball goes too far right, move right.

Before going any further a quick review is needed.

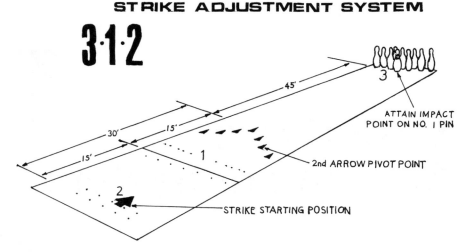

Figure 7.1 The 3-1-2 Strike Adjustment System (Courtesy of NBC).

- The head pin is on the 20th board.
- The 1-3 pocket is on the 17th board.
- The 3 pin is near the 14th board.
- The Brooklyn pocket is near the 23rd board.

With the above information in mind, the bowler can make adjustments by determining the number of boards separating the pocket from the actual point of contact of the ball. Specifically, this 3-1-2 system states, FOR EVERY 3 BOARDS THE BALL IS OFF AT THE PINS, MOVE THE FEET IN THE STANCE 2 BOARDS IN THE DIRECTION OF THE ERROR. (Figure 7.1)

SELF EVALUATION QUESTIONS

1. In a strike ball delivery, if the ball consistently goes left, which direction to you move in the stance? If it goes right?
2. How does the 3-1-2 system work?
3. The following are found on what boards?
   a. 1-3 pocket   c. 3 pin
   b. 1 pin   d. Brooklyn pocket

If the ball is properly delivered and rolls over the second arrow but strikes the head pin flush leaving big splits time after time, the following adjustment should be made. Knowing the head pin is on the 20th board and the 1-3 pocket is on the 17th board, the bowler is able to determine that this ball roll is three boards away from the pocket. Using the 3-1-2 formula, move the stance two boards to the left.

On another day or lane, the ball may be consistently entering the Brooklyn pocket. The Brooklyn pocket is six boards to the left of the 1-3 pocket so the needed adjustment to be made is moving the point of origin four boards to the left. And yet on the third day or lane, the ball may roll down the lane and contact the 3 pin flush, missing the head pin altogether. The 3 pin is approximately 3 boards away from the pocket, so the adjustment is made by moving the point of origin two boards to the right.

This adjustment system will work only when the bowler faces and walks toward the target arrow. This will result in the bowler walking at a slight angle and playing the lane on diagonals. Walking towards the target arrow will put the bowler in proper delivery position, and will prohibit the bowler from following-through with poor direction or dropping the shoulder in order to hit the target.

How does this system work mathematically? We have already established that it is 75 feet from the third row of locator dots to the head pin. The distance from the starting position to the target arrow (the pivot point) is approximately 30 feet. That leaves a 45 foot spread from the target arrow to the head pin, so the ball has another 15 feet further to roll. Putting this into a ratio, the stance to target ratio is 30 feet to 75 feet, with the target pin ratio at 45 feet to 75 feet. Breaking into smaller fractions, it is a ratio of 2/5th to 3/5th or 2:3. If the bowler makes a two board adjustment in the starting position, and the ball rolls across the same target arrow, the result is a three board change when the ball hits the pins. This is all due to the length of the lane involved and the distance between the starting position, the target, and the pins.

Once the bowler makes an adjustment, it is necesssary to turn the body and feet to face the target arrow and to walk toward it during the approach. This will result in a one board change (or adjustment) at the point of release at the foul line. It is 15 feet from the start to the foul line and another 15 feet from the foul line to the target. Thus, if the bowler, for example, adjusts two boards left in the stance, then the sliding foot at release point would actually be one board to the left of the old point of origin.

When using this system, one must heed a few words of advice. Don't make adjustments on the basis of one delivery or poor deliveries. Be certain that it was a good delivery and that it did go over the target arrow consistently. Don't confuse "pulling the ball" with too much hook; or following through toward the right with too little hook.

Additionally, keep in mind that this system works very well if making one or two adjustments (two to four board adjustment in the stance either left or right). However, if a third adjustment is attempted, the system tends to break down because at this point it becomes necessary to also make a target adjustment. Nevertheless, there should be no problem moving a total of four boards in either direction.

This system can also be used if the strike ball is hitting light (more on the 3 pin than the 1) or heavy (more on the 1 pin than the 3) by moving half the distance in the stance or one board. Again this follows the formula since this means the ball is hitting the pocket at the 15.5 board and the 18.5 board respectively. The error is one-half of the 3 board error or 1.5 off target. If the bowler uses ratio of 3:2, the feet would be adjusted 1 board in the stance.

SELF EVALUATION QUESTIONS

1. After your foot adjustments in the 3-1-2, in what direction do you take your approach?
2. What stance adjustments must be made if the strike ball consistently hits:
   a. Head pin   c. Heavy on the 1
   b. Heavy on the 3

IN A NUTSHELL

- The 3-1-2 strike adjustment system is mathematically formulated according to the dimensions of the lane.
- For every 3 boards the ball is off when it hits the pins, move 2 boards in the starting position.
- Move the stance in the direction of the error or mistake. If the ball goes too far to the right, move right or vice versa.
- With this stance, the body and feet must be square to the target, the intended line of ball roll, and *not* the foul line.
- This system only works within a four board stance adjustment in either direction.
- This system works in any proportion of the mathematical ratio.

8

The 3-6-9 Spare Conversion System

The 3-6-9 spare system is the most basic of all spare conversion systems. It has been scientifically developed for accuracy and uses a constant target for consistency and ease of learning. It is a system that takes the guesswork out of spare conversions.

Before this spare adjustment system can be implemented, the bowler must be cognizant of the following principles:

- The key pin must be identified in all spare conversion attempts.
- The basic rule of thumb for the commencement of the approach is to move to the side of the approach area opposite the location of the pins standing.
- All adjustments for pins remaining on the left of center are made from the correct point of origin for the strike ball delivery.
- All adjustments for pins remaining on the right of center are made from the correct point of origin for the 10 pin delivery.

The strike ball point of origin has been established in the previous chapter, so now we need to learn how to locate the key pin. The key pin is the pin one needs to hit in order for all other pins to fall. It is the only pin on which we focus our attention during a spare conversion. This pin in a two-pin leave is the pin closest to the bowler. In a three-pin cluster, it is the pin in the middle. If a baby split (where the ball can be fitted in between the two pins) it is the pin missing between the two pins left standing. If four or more pins are standing and the head pin is one of them, the head pin is the key pin. In a split where the pins are greater than 12 inches apart, the key pin is the pin, either real or imaginary, adjacent to the one closest to you on the outside of the combination. (Figure 8.1)

3-6-9 Spare Conversion System

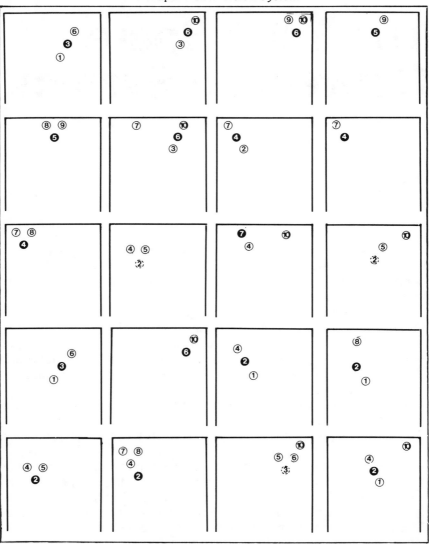

Figure 8.1 Identifying the key pin.

SELF EVALUATION QUESTION

What is the key pin in the following?
- a. 2-4-5   d. 9-10
- b. 1-3-6   e. 6-7-10
- c. 6-9-10   f. 2-4-7

In converting pins to the left of the head pin, the key pin must be located and then, using the rule of thumb, the feet will be moved right of the strike ball origin. For each pin to the left of the head pin, the feet will be moved three boards. (Figure 8.2). In order to convert the 2 pin, or any combination of the 2 pin (2-4-5, 2-8, 1-2-4, etc.), move the starting stance three boards to the right of the strike ball stance, aim for the second target arrow from the right, and walk towards the 2 pin slightly. The 2 pin, or any combination of the 2 pin, will not be covered by the ball providing the delivery is consistent.

To convert the 4 pin, or any 4 pin combination, the bowler must move six boards to the right of the strike ball stance, aim for the same second target arrow, and walk towards the 4 pin.

When the 7 pin is left standing, or when it is the key pin, the bowler will move nine boards to the right of the strike ball stance, aim for the second arrow, and walk towards the 7 pin. (Figure 8.3)

If the bowler walks towards the key pin, it will put the body at a slight angle to the foul line. This is the only way these spare adjustments will work properly. The shoulders are square to the target arrow and the key pin, not to the foul line.

The importance of delivering and rolling the ball the same way, over the same target arrow, changing the point of origin, cannot be overemphasized in the 3-6-9 system. This only changes the approach angle slightly and allows conversion of spares without changing the armswing or movement toward the foul line.

SELF EVALUATION QUESTION

Where will your point of origin be in order to convert the following key pins?
- a. 4 pin   c. 2 pin
- b. 7 pin   d. 8 pin

Conversion of right side spares uses the same theory as just discussed; however, the point of origin and the target changes. Instead of using the strike ball origin, one now adjusts from the 10 pin point of origin, always using the 3rd target arrow from the right. (Figure 8.4)

To find the point of origin for the 10 pin, the stance, using the left foot as a guide, should be at the place near the left edge of the lane, at least 15 boards left of center. Draw an imaginary line through the third

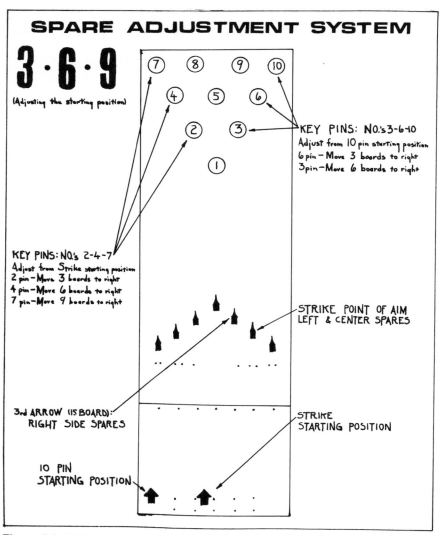

Figure 8.5 a) The 3-6-9 adjustment for the left-side spares b) The spare angle and target arrow used for the 10 pin c) The 3-6 adjustment made for right-side spares.

arrow from the right to the 10 pin. Still on the left, walk toward the 10 pin and deliver the ball in the same place. If the ball goes into the channel, move a board or two to the right. If the ball goes too far to the left of the 10 pin, move a board or two to the left. When the correct adjustments have been made, and when it is certain the right origin board has been found for the 10 pin, the spare adjustments for the other pins on the right of center may be made.

Figure 8.3 Picking up the 7 pin.   **Figure 8.4 Picking up the 10 pin.**

To convert the 6 pin, or any combination of the 6 pin, move three boards right of the 10 pin origin point, face the third target arrow, walk and swing toward the 6 pin.

For the 3 pin conversion, or any combination of the 3 pin, move six boards to the right of the 10 pin point of origin, face the target arrow, walk and swing toward the 3 pin. (Figure 8.5)

A spare conversion involving the 1 pin or the 5 pin is the basic strike ball. No adjustment from your strike ball point of origin or target is necessary

SELF EVALUATION QUESTION

Where will your point of origin be in order to convert the following pins?

   a. 3 pin   c. 10 pin
   b. 6 pin   d. 1 pin

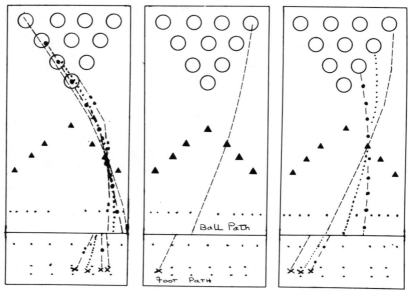

Figure 8.5 (a) The 3-6-9 adjustment for the left-side spares (b) The spare angle and target arrow used for the 10 pin (c) The 3-6 adjustment made for right-side spares.

By using this 3-6-9 formula, spare conversions become simple and almost automatic. Remember these basic points while using the 3-6-9 adjustment system:

- Locate the key pin.
- For spare leaves to the left of center, your point of aim is the second target arrow from the right. For spare leaves on the right, focus on the third target arrow from the right.
- For a leave to the left of center, adjust your starting position by moving 3, 6, or 9 boards to the right of your strike ball point of origin. Do this in accordance with your key pin.
- For a leave on the right side of lane, find the key pin and adjust to this pin by moving either 3 or 6 boards to the right of your 10 pin point of origin.
- Always walk toward the key pin and deliver the ball in the same manner as the strike ball. If delivered properly, the shoulders will be square to the target and not to the foul line.
- A left-hander employing the system would make all spare adjustments to the left from the strike point of origin or the 7 pin point of origin.

PART B

ADVANCED BOWLING

Sometimes an old habit needs to be broken in order to make room for a better habit. Alhtough any change may produce an initial feeling of being awkward and uncomfortable, the bowler should exercise patience and give the suggested improvements a chance to work.

9

Alternatives To The Four-Step Approach

For the purpose of establishing a common denominator in identifying an advanced bowler, we are making the assumption that advanced bowlers have a consistent and recognizable style and can carry an average over 140. Their experience gives them considerable background and knowledge.

Many times advanced bowlers hit a plateau and seem to be unable to raise their average. Since these bowlers have considerable experience in the game of bowling, and more than likely do many things well, they cannot erase their previous knowledge and start from scratch. Therefore, the next section of this text is devoted to improvements for advanced bowlers which should not destroy their existing game.

Suggested improvements, for the most part, will be minor; however, a few may be major. It should be noted that sometimes an old habit needs to be broken in order to make room for a better one. In such a case, the change may feel awkward and uncomfortable at first. Therefore, we urge the bowler to exercise patience and give suggested improvements a chance to work. Only then can the changes be reflected in improved scores.

After reaching a higher skill level, many bowlers start deviating from the norm and using techniques that seem to work best for them. They may vary the footwork patterns as well as their hand positions.

We intend to provide a thorough understanding of these variations and suggest ideas for bettering what has been established or suggest the easiest method of change.

FOOTWORK VARIATIONS

The 4-step approach is the most common of all footwork patterns mainly because it involves a natural rhythm where there is an arm motion for each foot motion. With this basic coordination, it is an easy and efficient approach to teach and to learn.

The first step of the 4-step approach is taken with the right foot for right-handers. Many bowlers have formed the habit of moving the arm and legs in opposition to one another and find it natural to step with the left foot. If this is the case, the bowler would develop a three, five, or seven-step approach.

Also, many bowlers feel the 4-step approach results in a choppy, robot-like movement, especially if they have learned it to a cadence of "one, two, three and slide" instead of the "shuffle-shuffle-shuffle-slide" approach.

Five-Step Approach

For many advanced bowlers, a 5-step approach is fairly common. This 5-step approach allows for a more natural start because the bowler will step with the left foot using the principle of opposition. The 5-step may also allow more time and distance in which to generate momentum on the ball. It gives the ball more time to move through the pendular swing.

The major disadvantage to this 5-step approach is the fact that there is not always a correlation between what the arms and feet are doing making it more difficult to teach and learn. A bowler may also feel he/she must "rush to the foul line" in order to coordinate the ball and the feet at delivery.

Actually, the 5-step is similar to the 4-step with the exception that the bowler's weight is on the right foot in the stance and the left foot will step out first. Consequently, there is an extra step in the beginning. The ball is still held to the right of the body in the stance but probably a little higher to allow for a little longer arc to take up the extra time of the extra step. (Figure 9.1)

The ball is still pushed out and down in the pushaway after the left foot moves to counteract the weight of the ball. In other words, the bowler takes a small step with the left foot, then moves the ball in the second step. (Figure 9.2) In contrast to the 4-step approach where the ball starts back on the *second* step, in the 5-step approach the ball is just starting into the backswing near the *third* step. With the additional length of the swing arc, the small extra step in the beginning should prevent any problems.

Figure 9.1 In a 5-step approach the ball is held higher in the stance.

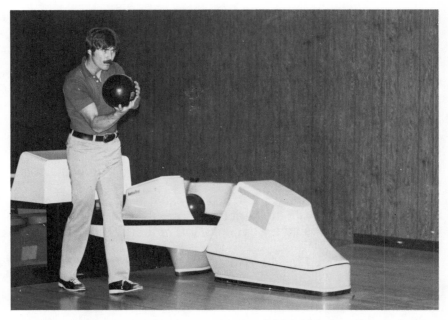

Figure 9.2 Taking a small first step with the right foot before the pushaway in the 5-step approach.

Three-Step Approach

It is not an absolute necessity that a 3-step approach be changed,but if timing problems are resulting from this approach, it is relatively easy to adopt the 4 or 5-step with minor adjustments.

The analysis of the timing in the 3-step finds the first step of this approach to be the same as the second step in the 4-step for the swing and approach coordination. Good 3-step timing should find the ball down by the left leg (first step), ready to go into the backswing of the arc. In order to do this, the bowler must have moved the ball out and down before the feet start the move into the approach. In accordance with the principle of balance we previously learned, the foot should move to maintain balance. If the foot moves too early in the 3-step approach, the bowler will be out of time. Most 3-step approach bowlers combat this problem by "muscling" the ball to make the swing fit the feet. The resulting steps are usually very large in order to give the ball a chance to complete the swing.

Maintaining a smooth 3-step approach means that the bowler must eliminate the "muscled" swing and hurried approach, take the stance closer to the foul line, and increase knee flexion to lower the center of gravity to lurching to the foul line.

No-Step Approach

Many children, senior citizens, and handicapped bowlers have found bowling a challenging and fun activity. Many become good bowlers even though they are unable to take an approach.

We have previously established that both the pendular swing and the approach generate the needed force required on the ball. If a bowler cannot take steps in the approach, more momentum must be generated in the swing. This can be accomplished by holding the ball fairly high in the stance at the foul line, concentrating on keeping the arm and elbow perfectly straight in the swing, and executing a complete follow through.

The follow through must come up and out at least to eye level and be perfectly straight with the target board or arrow. As always during the entire swing, absolute concentration is focused on the target board or arrow.

A lack of ball speed will result in a greater hook, thereby necessitating adjustments which were discussed in previous sections of this text. The bowler will probably need to stand left of center, rolling the ball further toward the right.

IN SUMMARY

- Once habits have been formed, they are more difficult to change. Changes usually feel awkward.
- Deviating from the norm in foot and hand position is not uncommon in advanced bowlers.
- The 4-step approach is usually recommended but bowlers may use others as long as flexibility, balance, and timing are still present.
- The major point to remember in all approaches is that the footwork is adjusted to the swing instead of the swing to the footwork.

Identifying their particular ball track will assist advanced bowlers in rolling a more effective ball.

10

Ball Tracks

In order to assist advanced bowlers in rolling a more effective ball, it is necessary to identify their particular ball track. The ball track is the pattern of "scratch marks" that develop on the surface of the ball. They represent the portion of the ball that touches the lane as it travels toward the pins. This is fairly easy to identify with a bowler who has his/her own ball. Due to the consistent and repetitious release of the ball, a series of nick marks will form on the surface of the ball where the ball consistently touches the lane. Another method of identifying the track is by observing the oil ring left on the ball or by putting a piece of tape on the ball and watching its rotation pattern as the ball travels down the lane. These wear marks or rotation patterns will usually be indicative of one of four ball tracks most commonly found in bowling today—the full roller, semi-roller, spinner, and reverse hook commonly referred to as a back-up ball.

It has been stressed throughout this book that the thumb should theoretically be at 10 o'clock at the release point. However, due to the weight of the ball or intended action of the fingers, the elbow will automatically rotate slightly either clockwise or counterclockwise, so the thumb should end up rotating to the position of 11 or 10 o'clock upon release.

IDENTIFICATION OF BALL TRACKS

Full Roller

The full roller ball track may be identified by the nick marks passing on the outside of the finger holes and the inside of the thumbhole, splitting the ball in half, rolling over the label of the ball. Since it is rolling around the 27-inch circumference of the ball, it is called a full roller.

In a full roller, the thumb rotates in a clockwise direction from 10 o'clock to 11 o'clock at the very last instance of release. The fingers lift through and impart a counterclockwise rotation on the ball. Thus, there are two rotations being placed on the ball, the primary rotation being the counterclockwise one as the fingers release. This is a result of the thumb coming out of the ball first and the fingers last. This release method is a very effective one and will enable the ball to hook from right to left for a right-hander. One of the characteristics of a full roller is the fine narrow track on the ball showing great consistency and accuracy, especially on the outside line.

The full roller is a good ball to deliver since it produces a right to left hooking action as it travels down the lane. The full roller enables a bowler to achieve a consistent and accurate type of release.

Often, it does have trouble carrying strikes because it has an "end over end" roll which results in the ball rolling right through the pin deck leaving many 4, 7, and 10 pins. It becomes an effective ball when rolled from an outside line.

Semi-Roller

The second common type of ball track is one where the nick marks pass on the outside of the finger holes and on the outside of the thumb hole. Obviously, this ball is rolling over a smaller portion of the ball instead of the full circumference so it is called a semi-foller or a ¾ roller.

The fingers lift through the ball also in a counter-clockwise direction. The nick marks may vary from being near the thumb hole or as far as two inches away.

The advantage of the semi-roller is that it has greater pin action than the other ball rolls because it has a great right to left hooking action. The heavier portion of the ball is heading toward the pocket as the ball travels down the lane. Upon pin contact, this heavier portion of the ball will help decrease the ball deflection and will drive the pins sideways, thus increasing the pin carry. Without a consistent approach, this ball roll may lose accuracy because of its increased hooking action.

Spinner

The spinner is considered an offshoot of the semi-roller. It is merely an overturned or an exaggerated semi-roller delivery where the thumb rotates too far counterclockwise, all the way from 11 o'clock toward 8 or 7 o'clock. The ball is actually spinning on a very small portion of the ball surface, reacting like a top going down the lane as it spins on its own axis. Often a spinner can be identified by watching the thumb of the bowler at the release. It will usually be pointing down.

The spinner hook travels down the lane in a fairly straight line. As it contacts the pins, it will bounce off in the opposite direction (maximum deflection), similar to the action of a spinning top hitting a wall. As it hits the pocket, it will deflect to the right leaving spare combinations which include the 5 pin. Due to its straight path, it may be a very effective and accurate ball on very dry lanes when most balls are hooking too much.

Backup Ball

The backup ball, or reverse hook, is basically an offshoot of the full roller. It hooks from left to right unlike the normal right left hook for right-handers. The thumb rotates clockwise from 10 to 12 o'clock which is an exaggeration of the full roller release. However, due to this exaggeration, the ball cannot receive a counterclockwise lift with the fingers.Consequently, the fingers continue a clockwise rotation through the release which brings about the left to right or reverse hooking action.

The backup ball, or reverse hook, is a totally ineffective ball unless the right-handed bowler moves to the left and rolls for the 1-2 pocket. There are three main reasons for this ineffectiveness:

1. It is inconsistent because it is difficult to regulate the excess clockwise rotation placed on the ball.
2. It may put undue strain on the wrist and elbow causing elbow soreness and tendonitis.
3. It has maximum pin deflection in the 1-3 pocket.

It is also difficult to roll from the left into the Brooklyn side (1-2 pocket) because of the inability to impart enough clockwise rotation and lift.

Thumper

Even though the thumper is not a recognized type of ball roll, occasionally this track will occur. A thumper merely finds the ball rolling over the thumb hole all the way down the lane. The thumper is usually caused by insufficient counterclockwise rotation of the fingers at the release point or by the thumb coming out of the thumb hole too early or too late.

In order to correct this error, the hand position needs to be changed in the stance by moving the thumb and fingers either more to the side of the ball or more underneath the ball (starting at 9 o'clock or 11 o'clock rather than 10 o'clock). The wrist should also be checked to make sure it is firm. If these two suggestions do not work, the ball balance should be checked.

CORRECTIONS AND CHANGES IN BALL TRACKS

The two most desirable ball tracks are the full roller and the semi-roller. It is not a must to change everyone's ball track to one of these two, however. It really depends upon the intention and intensity of the bowler. Many times they can be encouraged to change by showing the disadvantages of the ball they are currently rolling in comparison to the advantages of the full roller or semi-roller. However, change is sometimes painful because the bowler's average will fall and accuracy will definitely diminish during the learning phase.

Backup Ball

We have found that the backup ball is really an exaggerated full roller. When does a full roller become a backup? Remember, the fingers are lifting counterclockwise in the full roller but clockwise in the backup. This is caused by the thumb staying left of the 12 o'clock position on the ball. Basically, the 12 o'clock position is the cutoff point as to whether the ball becomes a full roller or a backup ball.

A backup ball delivery could easily be changed into a full roller and this sometimes may be accomplished merely by changing the thumb position in the stance from the 10 o'clock position to an 8 or 9 o'clock position. At the point of release, it will be near 12 o'clock resulting in a full roller rather than the 10 to 2 o'clock position, ending in a backup.

Once someone has been convinced to change from the backup ball to a more effective delivery, the following suggestions could be used to help in eliminating the backup bowler's habits:

- The bowler is assigned a new target (second arrow from the right) and a new starting position (right arm in line with the target arrow). It all looks and feels wrong to the bowler because he/she feels as though the lane itself is to the left.
- In the stance, the ball should be held off to the right side of the body with the wrist firm. Overemphasize the thumb and finger position by placing them at 9 and 3 o'clock. This exaggeration of hand placement is a teaching gimmick many use in order to

obtain the desired result. This is why the bowler may even be encouraged to place the hand at an 8 and 2 o'clock position.

- If these suggestions have been tried and the bowler still rolls a backup ball, check the direction of the pushaway. If he/she was used to holding the ball in front of the body rather than to the side, the pushaway probably went out to the right. If he/she continues to do this with the ball held off to the side, the result would be the ball swinging behind his/her back. Anytime the ball swings around the back, there is a tendency to compensate by coming through and rotating the elbow inside out which results in a backup.

A ball track is the pattern of "scratch marks" that develop on the surface of the ball. These marks represent the portion of the ball that touches the lane as it travels toward the pins.

- The next area to check is the knee flexion. If the bowler does not flex the knees and shuffle the feet in the approach, there is a tendency for the shoulder to drop. When the shoulder drops, the elbow rotates.
- If the backup still persists, the rotation of the elbow in the downswing should be checked. In a backup ball, the elbow will rotate inside out. For an exaggerated compensation, the inside of the elbow should be facing the body all of the time, thus placing the thumb at the 9 o'clock position.
- If the wrist rotates at the release point, direct the bowler to point his/her index finger at the target as he/she releases the ball.
- The balance of the ball and the pitch of the thumb hole may need to be checked.
- As a last resort, have the bowler convert to a semi-roller.

For those bowlers who do not want to change from a backup ball, more effective ball action may be obtained by developing maximum angle into the pocket. This can be done by adjusting the stance and target arrow so that the bowler is aiming high for the 18th board. The more common advice is to have the ball balanced as if it were drilled for a left-hander. This would increase the drive of the ball in the opposite direction as the bowler plays the left side of the lane and aims for the 1-2 pocket.

Full Roller

Many times a bowler rolling a full roller would like to increase the hook on the ball by increasing the lift and side rotation. This can be accomplished by placing the thumb at the 9 o'clock rather than the 10 o'clock position. This action will increase the thumb rotation, and therefore, increase the counter rotation of the fingers.

The second thing that could be done would be to pull the index finger closer to the gripping fingers and spread the little finger as far out as it will comfortably go. This will help increase the lift on the ball and allow the ball to finish more strongly into the pocket.

Semi-Roller

The changes for a semi-roller are quite opposite to those found in the full roller. Instead of starting with the thumb at 10 o'clock, place it at 12 o'clock with the hand underneath the ball. This will increase the side rotation and lift applied to the ball because of the increased rotation of the fingers at release.

Secondly, the fingers should be adjusted by spreading the index finger out and away from the gripping fingers while pulling the little finger in closer. This action will help to impart a stronger counterclockwise rotation at release point.

In the case of a very slow lane where too much hook is a problem, a bowler could *decrease* side rotation and hook by simply reversing those actions designed to increase side rotation as stated in the previous section on the full- roller and above on the semi- roller.

Spinner

It is recommended that an effective spinner be converted to a semi-roller since the spinner is an overturned or exaggerated semi-roller. This can easily be accomplished by making sure the wrist is extended and the hand is underneath the weight of the ball. The bowler should attempt to maintain this 2 o'clock position during the release. This action will insure the release of the thumb from the thumb hole prior to that of the fingers. The bowler should be reminded that at the release he/she should curl the fingers into the palm of the hand with the the thumb up.

It is recommended that if someone refuses to change from a spinner, he/she stand farther right and get maximum ball angle upon the entry into the pocket for better pin action and less deflection.

TEACHING CUES

- To correct a spinner, have the student start with the thumb at 12 or 1 o'clock. Concentrate on keeping the elbow close to the hip during the swing and attempt to release the ball with the thumb at 12 o'clock (an over-exaggeration). Visualize attempting to roll a straight or backup ball. This will result in a semi-roller.

- In order to create a full roller from a backup ball, have the bowler start the thumb at 8 or 9 o'clock. During the swing, keep the inside of the elbow facing toward the body in order to keep the thumb in a downward position throughout the swing.

IN SUMMARY

Changes should be made in the ball tracks only when the ball track presently rolled has been properly identified. The prescription changes are unique to each ball roll pattern.

Methods of identifying ball tracks:

- By the nick marks scarred into the ball surface.
- By the oil ring left on the ball.
- By putting a tracer on the ball and watching its action.

   1. In a full roller, this tracer would roll very high and end over end while angled to the left.
   2. In a semi-roller, it would roll in a much tighter circle on the left.
   3. In a spinner, it would be in a very tiny compact roll or going

around in a Saturn-type ring, or almost stationary on top of the ball.

4. In a backup, the tracer would be rolling on the right side of the ball.

11

Weights and Ball Balances

Many bowlers will weight their balls differently in order to assist in making their balls roll more or less, hook earlier or later. There are basically four kinds of weighting systems or imbalances that can be found in bowling balls—top weight, side weight, finger weight, and thumb weight.

TOP WEIGHT

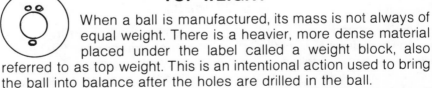

When a ball is manufactured, its mass is not always of equal weight. There is a heavier, more dense material placed under the label called a weight block, also referred to as top weight. This is an intentional action used to bring the ball into balance after the holes are drilled in the ball.

By looking at the ball, one cannot tell how much top weight the ball has. When a ball is purchased, an accompanying tag on the box gives information, i.e. fourteen pounds, two ounces, 4T. The 4T informs the purchaser that before the ball is drilled, the ball has four ounces of top weight. Consequently, when the three holes are drilled, one and a half to two ounces of ball material is removed which leaves approximately two ounces of top weight. According to the American Bowling Congress, a legal ball may not have more than three ounces of top weight after drilling.

Top weight generally gives the ball some extra hitting power. The more top weight in the ball, the greater the skid of the ball and conversely, the less the top weight, the earlier the ball rolls.

Effect of Top Weight on a Full Roller

Generally speaking, a bowler rolling a full roller should keep the top weight at one and a half ounces or less. As a full roller tracks across the ball's label, the ball will start pulsating or loping in a flywheel effect if there is too much top weight. This will result in a lopsided and ineffective roll.

Effect of Top Weight on a Semi-Roller

A bowler delivering a semi-roller can easily vary the amount of weight on the ball to achieve the desired effect. The top weight will place an imbalance in semi-roller ball by placing more weight on the larger portion of the ball. The imbalance causes the heavier portion of the ball to always hook towards the pocket resulting in better pin action.

Lane Conditions and Top Weight

If the lanes are dry or hooking, more top weight would help delay the hook of the ball. Generally, if the lanes are oily, less top weight would help the ball pick up an earlier roll and skid somewhat less. These basic rules may vary depending on how near the track is to the thumb hole.

SIDE WEIGHT

This second type of ball weighting is achieved by drilling the holes toward either side of the label rather than centered on the label. The holes can be drilled to the left (positive side weight) or to the right (negative side weight). After drilling, a ball is allowed to have a maximum of one ounce of side weight. The result is, in effect, a ball with one side slightly heavier than the other.

When a bowler releases a ball with a positive side weight, the heavier portion of the ball is always hooking towards the pocket so this imbalance may help the ball to hook. However, the more side weight put in a ball, the further the ball will tend to skid.

A popular drilling position for today's lane conditions is to drill the holes to the right side of the label. This is called negative side weight. This negative side weight characteristically helps the ball go into an earlier roll and then continue to roll in a true arc. However, if there is too much negative side weight, the ball will not finish into the pocket because the heavier portion of the ball is rolling away from the pocket. Under certain playing conditions, negative side weight will hold the line much better.

FINGER WEIGHT

The third type of weighting is called finger weight and can be identified by the finger holes being drilled close to the label and the thumb further from the label. The maximum legal finger weight after; the ball is drilled is one ounce.

Characteristically, this imbalance helps the ball to skid further and hook later, but when it hooks, it will hook more sharply. It is very effective when the lanes are quite dry and a longer skid is desired.

THUMB WEIGHT

Thumb weight is the opposite of finger weight. One can recognize this weight by observing the thumb hole drilled closer to the label and the label and the fingers farther from it. Again, there is a one ounce maximum.

Basically, this thumb weight helps the ball to go into an earlier roll and start the hook earlier. It is used very effectively on oily or fast lanes.

SUMMARY

Weight blocks are usually placed in bowling balls to balance the ball after ball material is removed by the drilling process. However, many bowlers desire various kinds of weight imbalance in order to minimize or maximize the amount of skid, roll, and hook in order to adjust to various lane conditions.

It is possible for a single bowling ball to have any combination of varying weight amounts. However, a ball could not have finger and thumb weight nor positive and negative side weight at the same time, but all other combinations or degrees are possible and widely used.

A bowled ball is most effective when it travels at an average speed of 17 miles per hour with the right amount of forward roll and side rotation.

12

Lift and Revolutions

Previously, we learned that the ball is most effective when it travels at an average speed of 17 miles per hour with the right amount of forward roll and side rotation. "Lift," which is imparted on the ball at the release, produces the forward revolutions and accentuates the side rotation on the ball. "Lift" is the pressure a bowler feels on his/her fingertips at the release point after the thumb has been removed from the ball. It is the resistance created when the weight of the ball, which is a downward force, meets the resistance of the fingers moving in an upward direction. The action of the thumb and fingers at the release finds the thumb coming out at the bottom of the swing and the fingers remaining for a split second longer into the upswing phase of the arc. This is the point at which "lift" is developed and felt.

Since it is nearly impossible to practice "lift" by itself, several conscious acts an can be practiced to get "lift" to happen more automatically and consistently.

- The body should arrive at the foul line a split second before the ball. This will put the body in a "set" position and the ball can come through with maximum leverage on the hand underneath the weight of the ball.
- The vertical balance line must be perfectly positioned over the bent forward knee in order to impart effective lift on the ball. In any other position, the hand will not be underneath the weight of the ball.

- A good horizontal balance line must be achieved by counter balancing the weight of the ball on the right with the extension of body parts on the left.
- The ball must be as close as possible to the left (forward) ankle to impart "lift." This distance is usually about two to four inches from the outside of the ball since it would be quite difficult to impart lift on an object two feet away from the vertical line of the body. (Figure 5.3). (In Chapter 5 — this picture shows the ball in relation to the ankle upon delivery)
- The last step must be varied a bit from the norm by stepping slightly into the ball bath. This brings the ball closer to the left ankle.

At the release, it is a necessity to get maximum "feel" of the ball. Three suggestions are given here on how to increase this control factor:

- Concentrate on obtaining a feeling of the ball rolling off the hand.
- Practice squeezing the ball with the fingers while relaxing the thumb at the point of release.
- Curl the fingers into the palm of the hand at the release. (Figure 4.18).

REVOLUTIONS

The product of "lift" is counterclockwise revolutions or turn of the ball (right-handers). This is due to the application of the lifting pressure off the ball's center of gravity. An effective ball roll will have at least ten to twelve revolutions as it travels toward the pins. It is possible to achieve twelve to fourteen revolutions without compensating in the delivery. The closer a bowler can get to this number of revolutions, the more effective the ball becomes.

13

3-4-5 Strike Adjustment System

The 3-4-5 strike adjustment system is used by the more advanced bowler who has the ability to aim for and hit a *specific board* on the lane. This strike adjustment is used when the bowler is experiencing difficulty in "Carrying" strikes even though the ball is entering the pocket. The aim is accurate but the missing ingredient is appropriate angle of entry into the pocket. This 3-4-5 strike adjustment system will increase or decrease the angle into the pocket.

In this system, the pivot point or constant is the pocket, since the bowler has already established the correct impact point on the head pin but is seeking the correct impact point on the 3 pin. In adjusting for a better angle of entry, the bowler must make a change in the starting position and the target. Both the starting position and the target will be moved at the same time and in the same direction.

The proportions for the 3-4-5 adjustment are — for every five boards the feet are moved in the stance, the target is moved three boards. Again, using mathematical ratio, this system will work across the lane in either direction as long as the movement is five boards for the stance and three boards for the target. Remember, it is 75 feet from the third row of locator dots, 45 feet from the targets, and 60 feet from the foul line to the head pin. The ratio of the locator dots and the target arrows in relation to the total length of the lane is 5:3. (Figure 13.1)

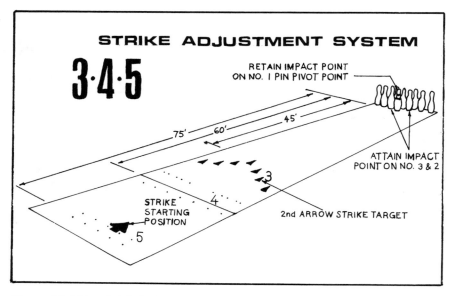

Figure 13.1 The 3-4-5 Strike Adjustment System (Courtesy of NBC)

The following guidelines should be used in implementing the 3-4-5 system. If the ball is entering the pocket heavy or at too much angle, adjust left. If you are hitting light in the pocket or at too little angle, move right. If the pin leaves consistently involve the 4 pin, or the 4-7 and 4-9 combinations, the ball is driving through the pocket too strongly, so the adjustment would be toward the left. Specifically, the move would be five boards to the left in the stance and three boards to the left with the target. The results will be the ball hitting the pocket at a decreased (flatter) angle.

If the ball enters the pocket but is consistently leaving the 5 pin, 5-7, 8-10, or 2-4-5 pin combinations, the reverse situation is occurring. The ball is hitting the pocket light with too little angle. The adjustment would be to move the starting position five boards to the right. The result will be the ball entering the pocket with a greater angle.

If the adjustment is insufficient and the situation continues, a good bowler will keep moving and adjusting. The ball will still contact the 1-3 pocket, but the entry will be at a different angle.

This system should work regardless of the target that is being used for the strike line and because the mathematical makeup will work in any proportion. It can be doubled (10:6) for a larger adjustment or cut in half (2.5:1.5) for minor adjustment.

SELF EVALUATION QUESTION

If a bowler is using the second arrow as the strike target but is leaving the following pins, what adjustment should be made?

a. 4 pin   c. 5-7
b. 5 pin   d. 4-7

IN SUMMARY

- The 3-4-5 system is used by advanced bowlers who are consistently hitting the pocket but not carrying strikes.
- This system merely changes the bowling ball's angle of entry into the pocket without affecting the accuracy.
- The pivot point is the pocket, making it necessary to make two adjustments—one with the feet and the other with the target.
- The rules governing this mathematical ratio are:
  1. For every five boards the feet move, the target is moved three boards.
  2. Both the feet and the target move in the same direction.
  3. If the ball is hitting heavy, move left.
  4. If the ball is hitting light, move right.
- The 5:3 ratio may be doubled or cut in half and used successfully since it is mathematically based.
- The system will work regardless of what strike line is used, and will not break down regardless of the number of moves.
- Remember, once an adjustment is made, the bowler must turn the body and the feet to face and walk toward the target.

To use the 2-4-6 spare adjustment system, the bowler must have developed enough accuracy and consistency so that he/she can adjust and hit a specific board rather than a large target arrow, since the target board will change.

14

2-4-6 Spare Adjustment System

Advanced bowlers often adopt the 2-4-6 spare adjustment system instead of the 3-6-9 system, especially when playing an inside or outside strike line. Playing an inside line means that the bowler is using a strike target to the left of the second arrow; playing to the right of the second arrow would be an outside line. The 3-6-9 system is of greater advantage for beginners whose target is basically the second arrow of somewhere between the eight and twelfth board. However, it does have limitations and starts to break down if the target moves from this area.

To use this system, the bowler must have developed enough accuracy and consistency so that he/she can adjust and hit a specific board rather than a large target arrow, since the target board will change. Instead of the pivot point or constant being the target arrow, the constant now becomes the stance position of the bowler. The bowler will have two starting positions on the approach when using the 2-4-6 system. One will be the strike position which will be used for all spares standing in the center and on the left side of the lane. The second starting position (10 pin starting position) will be established for rolling at pins on the right side of the lane. So instead of moving the starting position as in the 3-6-9 system, the bowler is now going to shift the target.

The basic rule of thumb for the 2-4-6 system states that when a spare adjustment is necessary, the spare target will be moved left of the strike target in increments of two boards. (Figure 14.1).

For all spares in the center where the key pin is the 1 or the 5 pin, the bowler stands in the strike starting position and rolls over the strike board or target.

For all spares on the left (2, 4, 7, or 8 as key pins), the stance is still the strike starting position but the target will shift to the left two boards for each pin to the left of the head pin. If the bowler leaves any spare combinations where the key pin is the 2 pin, the bowler will stand in the strike position and if he/she was using the second arrow as the target (10th board), he/she was using the second arrow as the target (10th board), he/she would move the target two boards to the left (12th board). Whereas, if the bowler leaves a 4 pin, he/she will stay in the same strike starting position but roll the ball four boards to the left of the strike board (14th board). If the key pin is the 7 pin, the bowler would move the target six boards left of the strike board (16th board.)

The only way the spare and strike systems will work consistently is if the bowler points the toes toward the key pin and walks toward that key pin and the target. If this rule is followed, the 2-4-6 spare adjustment system will work regardless of which board is used as the strike target.

SELF EVALUATION QUESTION

If the bowler is using the fifth board as the strike target, at which board will he/she be aiming for the following spare leaves:
  a. 2 pin   d. 7 pin
  b. 5 pin   e. 2-4-10
  c. 4-7 pin   f. 2-4-5

For all spares on the right, as in the 3-6-9 system, the bowler must find the 10 pin starting position through trial and error. It should be noted that if the bowler has been using the 3-6-9 system, this would be the same starting position. In searching for the exact 10 pin starting location, the third arrow should always be used for the target arrow. The basic rule still applies which is that you start from the left in order to roll for pins on the right.

After the 10 pin starting position has been determined, it will be used for all right side spares. If the 6 pin is left, the target is moved two boards to the left of the third arrow (17th board). In order to pick up the 3 or 9 pin from this same starting position, move the target four boards to the left of the third arrow (19th board).

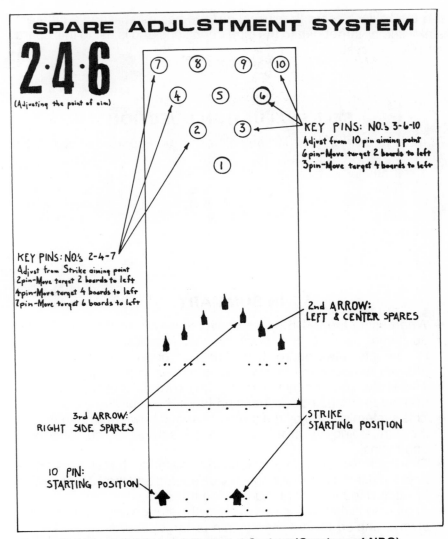

Figure 14.1 The 2-4-6 Spare Adjustment System (Courtesy of NBC)

It is a must to find the strike target, the strike starting position, and the 10 pin starting position before one can use this system effectively. This may explain why professional bowlers may sometimes bowl from the extreme right (an outside line) and other times from the left (an inside line). More than likely he/she has established a different strike line or target due to the lane conditions and is using this spare conversion system.

SELF EVALUATION QUESTION

In order to pick-up the following pins, at which board will the bowler aim?

a. 10 pin   d. 9 pin
b. 6 pin   e. 3-6-7
c. 3 pin   f. 6-9

IN SUMMARY

- When using the 2-4-6 spare conversion system, the two starting positions become the pivot points. The target is moved in increments of two boards to the left in accordance with the key pin. (For left-handers, the target always moves to the right.)
- This system is used by those who have a consistent approach and can place the ball over specified target boards.
- This system is used by the more advanced bowlers who may vary the strike line in order to take advantage of specific lane conditions.
- There are two starting positions in this stance, the strike starting position used for center and left side spares and the 10 pin starting position used in converting pins on the right.
- At all times when using this system, the stance and approach are always angled toward the key pin or target board.

15

Competitive Bowling

PHILOSOPHY OF COMPETITION

An early establishment of basic philosophy and objectives leads to success in any endeavor. Competitive bowling is no exception. The coach and each individual bowler should identify his/her own philosophy of competition and respective goals in order to plan a systematic course for achievement of those goals.

At the same time, however, a competitior should not lose sight of another very important objective—that of enjoyment.

The sections which follow will provide additional suggestions for goal achievement and help make your coaching responsibilities more enjoyable and successful.

PSYCHOLOGY OF COMPETITION

Once the technical fundamentals have been refined to successful habits, the game of bowling becomes more of a mental challenge. Almost 80 per cent of continued success is attributable to *concentration* and one's ability to determine and adjust to the subtle variations in concitions.

The bowler must be able to *"feel"* the momentum and *"sense"* the swing of the ball, even while under much pressure. Going for the fourth or fifth strike in a row should be just the same as trying for the first one, but it seldom is. Subtle tension and pressure, not to mention mechanical variations, must be detected and neutralized. Concentration is the name of the game!

Concentration is an awareness of self in the required movement and the absence of outside thoughts. During competition, we should react almost automatically and continually readjust, relying upon the ingrained motor patterns already established. The bowler should be aware of the target and the objective, without cluttering the mind with outside distractions.

Another important element is the ability to isolate events. Take one ball at a time, not the entire frame, the game, event, or outcome. A series of good individual shots creates a good game and a winning performance. A good bowler can immediately leave an error behind and look to the next ball.

Many sports participants attribute success or failure to luck, when in truth, luck is a minor factor. We must strive to minimize the effect of luck by making cool, logical adjustments. Luck will even itself out if we minimize its impact by the strength of our performance.

The bowler who can control his/her emotions and direct his/her attention and energies to the task at hand will find the greatest success. A calm assurance is an effective approach to the game. Getting upset or angry does not enhance performance and will only insure a loss of concentration and a probable series of poor shots.

Another key to the success of many bowlers, and other sports participants as well, is the ability to visualize the proper execution of the skill involved. The benefit of mental practice cannot be denied. Being able to visualize the perfect strike ball delivery while waiting for your turn to bowl can help your concentration and add to your effect-iveness at the same time.

All too many competitors make the very serious mistake of competing against someone on the other lane or the other team. A far better idea is to forget your opponents, their success and their mistakes, and bowl against yourself. This way, you spend your time concentrating on your own game rather than defending against your opponents' game. If you are evenly matched and you are bowling against yourself while your opponents are bowling against you, chances are that 90 per cent of the time you wll win!

The successful bowler must also find a degree of competitive relaxation. That is to say, confidence and concentration are the tools with which to combat nervous tension and pressure attendant to competition. We need to have a confident and positive attitude toward the event to allow for maximum effectiveness.

One final note—"losers" have a real fear of failure and therefore almost always anticipate it. Winners, on the other hand, use small setbacks as stepping stones for improvement and eventual success. Losing is not to be feared, not even considered, in the winner's search for success. One of the greatest lessons in winning is to learn not to defeat yourself. To succeed, one must eliminate the fear of failure, take the game of bowling one delivery at a time, and concentrate on your own performance. Remember the winner's attitude is one of "I will," and the loser continues to say "I can't."

COACHING IDEAS

The duty of a coach is to assist the athlete or performer in achieving optimal success in the pursuit of excellence. In order to achieve this objective, a bowling coach must organize individualized practices. Each individual should be aware of the goals and objectives of each practice session for meaningful and productive practice to take place.

The following are some suggestions on how to approach the coaching of bowling and the conducting of practices:

- Remember you are a coach/teacher and not a participant. Your duty is to assist each of the bowlers, rather than to improve upon your game.
- Know your bowling fundamentals and materials. Respect for you as a coach only can be obtained if the coach knows what he/she is talking about.
- Praise first and then present constructive criticism. Try to present everything in a positive manner.
- Give only one or two corrections at a time. If a coach over-instructs and gives the bowler too many things to think about at once, very little will be accomplished.
- Show enthusiasm and positivism. Both of these are contagious and will assist in fun and productive practices.
- While observing, make sure you are in the most advantageous position:
  1. On the ball side of the apporach
  2. Directly behind the ball swing
  3. At the foul line
  In front of the bowler on the lane
- Observe things in sequence. Move from the stance through the movements ending at the foul line and not vice versa. Many times corrections in the stance automatically make corrections occur in other areas.
- Don't be afraid to over-exaggerate the correction.
- Constant repetition enhances learning.
- Always look for the cause of the problem rather than trying to remedy the symptom.
- It will take between two to five games to establish a new pattern

providing the bowler is aware of the corrections on every shot.
- Individualize the practices.
- Make the other team members aware of each bowler's faults and errors. At some crucial time they may have to help that bowler.
- During practice, stress complete concentration. Don't allow "horseplay."
- Practice in the same type of clothing each individual will be wearing during competition.
- It is sometimes advantageous to practice in a match game situation, one against another.
- Develop ways to motivate each individual to want ultimate success.
- Work toward team rapport and team cohesiveness.
- Use visual playback methods whenever possible.
- Eliminate the fear of failure. Emphasize that a loss is merely a temporary setback. The winners motto is: "I can" and "we will."

LANE CONDITIONS

One of the most crucial variables a bowler must deal with is the variation in lane conditions from lane to lane, day to day, and from one establishment to another. Lane conditions will even change from the start of a bowling session to the end. Being able to adjust to the changing conditions will most often spell the difference between a good and a poor performance. Since we have previously indicated several adjustment systems, a little information on lane conditions may prove helpful.

As you may guess, the gowling lane surface is subject to a considerable amount of daily "wear and tear." In order to minimize the "wear and tear," to equalize lane conditions, and to prevent damage to the surface of the lanes, bowling establishments see to it that the lanes are carefully maintained. Most establishments care for their lanes on a daily basis. In addition to frequent "sweeping" with an oil coated mop, a very thin coat of oil based "dressing" is applied to the lane surface. This helps protrect the lane surface from the balls traveling on it, somewhat as motor oil protects a car's engine.

Based on the amount of daily play, bowling lanes need resurfacing from time to time. This process involves removal of all dressing and finish by sanding down the lane to make it perfectly level. All dents, ball tracks, and imperfections are removed in this sanding phase.

The next step is the application of a urethane, water-based, or lacquer finish applied directly to the bare wood. This is allowed to dry and harden, and then the final top dressing is applied as mentioned above.

There are many methods of oiling, varying amounts of oil, and many patterns of application, all helping to determine the lane conditions to which the bowler must adjust. The greater the quantity of oil, the more the ball tends to skid. Because of the skid, the ball will not "grab" soon enough for proper angle entry into the pins. This is usually called a "fast" or holding lane.

The lane with less oil, called a "slow" or hooking lane, allows the ball to hook more, as it skids less and begins to roll sooner on the lane. The angle of entry into the pocket generally needs to be decreased by the bowler on this type of lane.

Many advanced bowlers do not always play the second arrow strike line because of these varying lane conditions. They may decide lane conditions dictate an "inside line" (15th board or so) to decrease entry angle, or on slow lanes or an "outside line" to compensate for less hooking action on fast lanes.

It is the bowler's ability to adapt to changing lane conditions which will determine the eventual game score. This process is called "reading the lane" to determine just what adjustments in the target or the stance may be necessary. It must be rememberd that the approach, arm swing, and delivery should remain consistent no matter what the lane conditions are like. The correct adjustment to the appropriate strike line will mean the difference between a frustrating and successful performance.

HOW TO PRACTICE

In all sports, we equate practice with repetition of the actual game process. Bowling is no different. We say we are practicing when, in fact, we are bowling for score rather than improving various elements of our game.

The following suggestions are provided in an attempt to make practice sessions more productive in contributing to improvement and refining very specific techniques:

- Don't keep score.
- Roll your second ball first, shoot for a 7 pin or a 10 pin, then roll your strike ball.
- Practice for a particular reason, such as making a correction or change.
- Concentrate on only one or two things in a given practice session.
- Over-exaggerate your corrections at first until they become natural.
- Don't be excited about strikes.
- Be happy with making a satisfactory change in your game even though there may not be an immediate result.

- Make use of the "shadow bowling" capability of some lanes. The house also may be able to supply "dummy" rubber or paper pins to allow you to concentrate on one pin repeatedly.
- Practice with a knowledgeable buddy who can correctly assist you in diagnosing your progress on those one or two factors.
- Practice your concentration.
- Go to a quiet area with the fewest number of distractions and interruptions.
- If available, videotape or movie feedback provides an excellent resource for error analysis and correction.
- Give new techniques a chance to work. Don't expect miracles overnight.
- Remember, concentrated practice sessions can be enhanced by effective mental practice.
- Maintain your confidence. Don't give up on a new idea too soon.

APPENDICES

Appendix A

Scoring

The game or line of bowling consists of 10 frames. A bowler gets a maximum of two ball deliveries in each frame to knock all of the pins down. A perfect 300 game is scored by knocking all of the pins down with the first ball roll of each frame.

A typical scoresheet used in bowling is divided into the 10 frames. An accumulation score of each frame is kept in order to come up with the final game score. In the top right corner of each frame is a pair of small boxes, one for each ball roll.

The pinfall on each ball delivery is entered in the little boxes. If a bowler knocks down 7 pins on the first delivery, a 7 is placed in the first box.

If on the second ball, the bowler knocks 2 of the remaining 3 pins down, the 2 is placed in the second little box and the total fall for both balls is recorded in the frame.

If the bowler knocks down all of the pins in a frame in *two* deliveries, a spare is the result and is recorded by placing a diagonal slash (/) in the second little box.

In order to score a spare, the bowler will receive the 10 pins knocked down in that frame plus the pinfall of the next single ball delivery.

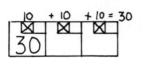 If a bowler knocks down all the pins with the first ball, it is called a strike and is recorded in the first little box as an X. In case of a strike, the second ball is not needed since all of the pins are already knocked down. A bowler who is credited with a strike gets to score the 10 pins he/she knocked down with that ball plus a bonus of the pinfall on the next two deliveries. Therefore, if a strike is recorded, nothing is placed in that frame until that bowler's turn comes up again and he/she rolls the next two balls for the next frame or frames.

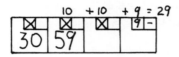 If the bowler records two strikes in a row, it is called a "double." In order to figure the pin count, follow the rule of 10 plus the next two balls. In this case, count the ten pin knocked down by the strike ball, the ten on the first bonus ball, and the eight on the second bonus ball.

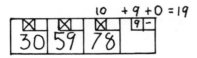 If a bowler rolls three strikes in a row, it is called a triple or a "turkey." Again, follow the rule of the 10 plus the pin count from the next two ball rolls which will result in a total of 30.

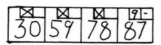 Then using the same formula figure the score for a double and add to the previous frame score.

 Now figure the score for the single strike left.

 And finally, add the 9 pin count for the next frame.

 If a bowler fails to knock any pins down on a ball roll, a miss (-) is recorded in the respective corner square.

When the pins left following the first delivery constitute a split, a circle is drawn around the number of pins knocked down on that delivery. The pins knocked down on the second ball roll are still recorded in the little right hand box.

If a bowler fouls on the first delivery of a frame, an F is recorded in the first little box and no pinfall is counted. All of the pins are reset for the second ball delivery. Only the pins knocked down with the second ball are counted, in this case 6 pins were knocked down.

If after knocking down pins on the first ball of a frame a foul is made, an F is recorded in the second little box and only the pinfall of the first ball delivery is counted in that frame.

The tenth frame is the final frame of the game. It is scored exactly as the previously scored frames unless a strike or spare occurs. When a spare occurs in the 10th frame, one bonus ball must be rolled in order to find out how much the spare scores. In this case, 10 (the pins knocked down in the spare) plus the 8 pins knocked down with the bonus ball. The 18 pin count is then added to the total in the 9th frame and placed in the 10th. THAT IS THE END OF THE GAME.

When a strike is recorded in the 10th frame, the bowler must roll two more balls in order to find out how much that strike scores. The score for the last strike (18) is added to the 9th frame score. The total score placed in the 10th frame is the score of the game and the pinfall from the extra two ball rolls is not added on.

The total column at the end of each line is used to total accumulated game scores. This score constitutes the bowler's series score.

Here is an example of an individual game:

HOW TO CALCULATE AN AVERAGE

If the total series is divided by the number of games bowled, the bowler's average for the series is obtained, i.e. 363 - : 3 = 121. During a competitive season, a bowler keeps a running account of his/her current average. This is accomplished by keeping track of each game bowled and adding it to the cumulative total of games previously bowled. By continually totaling and dividing the total by the number of games bowled, the bowler will find his/her current average. Any extra pins left over (fractions) are dropped from the average.

```
124
136
103
100
152
134
169
122
180
─────
1220 ÷9 = 135.55 = 135 average
```

Appendix B

League Bowling

HANDICAPPING

There are basically two major kinds of leagues in bowling, the scratch league and the handicap league. The scratch league merely means the actual scores rolled by the bowler are the scores used in competition. There is no means of equalizing the scores of the bowlers by giving pins to the less skilled bowler.

The handicap league "gives" pins to less skilled bowlers in order to equalize abilities, thus providing better, closer competition. Each league establishes its own handicap formula to be used throughout the season.

There are two main kinds of handicapping, the individual base handicap and the team base handicap. Each league will decide which of these styles of handicapping will be used as well as what base and percentage to use.

The Base Score

The base from which a handicap is figures is usually established by looking at the league's top bowler(s). The base should usually be a little above the top bowler(s) in the league. For leagues with bowlers who average in the 180's and 190's, a 200 base is commonly established. This basically means that a 200 average bowler would be bowling scratch, no handicap. Any bowler under a 200 would get a percentage of the pin difference between his/her average and the handicap base. In a lesser skilled league where the top bowler(s) does not exceed the average of 170 or so, a 180 base may be selected.

The Selected Percentage

To merely subtract a bowler's average from the base score would not be quite fair. So a designated percentage of the difference between the bowler's average and the base score is identified. The most common percentages are probably 75 and 80 percent, but they may range from 60 to 100.

Figuring Individual Based Handicaps

Some leagues will require that the handicap be figured for each individual on the team. Suppose the league has selected a base score of 180 and an 80 percent handicap figure, the following procedure would be followed to find Sam's handicap per game when he has an average of 140.

Subtract Sam's average from the base score.
Then take 80 percent of that score.
For each game Sam rolls, 32 pins will be added to his score.

```
   180
  -140
  ─────
    40
  ×.80
  ─────
 32.00
```

In order to find a team's handicap for each game using this system, each team member's handicap is figured as was Sam's, and added together.

		Individual Handicap
Example:	Sam	32
	Jane	40
	Tony	14
	Sue	10
	Jerry	12
		108 pins

This team would have a team handicap of 108 pins per game.

Team Base Handicapping

Sometimes it is more convenient to figure the total team handicap all in a single calculation rather than five separate calculations for each of the team members. This is accomplished by finding the team base by multiplying the 180 base score by the number of team members (180×5=900). This team base score, once found, will remain 900 throughout the season.

Now add all of the team member's averages together, subtract that total from the team base of 900 and take 80 percent of the difference.

		Average	
Example:	Sam	140	900 Team Base
	Jane	130	−765 Team Total Average
	Tony	162	
			————
	Sue	168	135
	Jerry	165	×.80 (Percentage)
		————	————
		765	108.00 Pins

Each week the handicap will differ from the week before because the individual averages will change.

FIGURING MARKS

In competitive bowling, a player or a team is interested in knowing the status of its score in relation to its opponents' as the game progresses. Instead of totaling each frame, an easy system has been worked out where marks are counted. A strike or a spare is usually referred to as a mark and each mark is worth a value of 10 pins. By counting the marks in each frame and keeping a running total, the bowler can tell approximately how many pins ahead or behind he/she is in that game.

Example:

TEAM A

	1	2	3	4	5	6	7	8	9	10
Frame	9 -	5 /	6 2	7 2	F 8	9 /	X	8 1	6 2 X 3 6	
Score	9	25	33	42	50	70	89	98	106	125	125
Frame	X	8 1	6 -	X	X	8 -	8 1	5 2	X 7 / 8	
Score	19	28	34	62	80	88	97	104	124	142	267
(MARKS)	1	2	-	3 + 1	5	6	7	-	8	10

TEAM B

Frame	6 2	9 -	6 /	8 -	X	4 5	8 /	5 3	F 6 9 -	
Score	8	17	35	43	62	71	86	94	100	109	109
Frame	6 3	2 /	8 -	X	3 3	9 -	4 /	8 -	X 5 / 6	
Score	9	27	35	51	57	66	84	92	112	128	237
(MARKS)	1	2	3	4	-	6	-	7	8

By examining the marks in frame 2, Team A has one mark more than Team B which is approximately 10 pins. In the 7th frame, Team A has 7 to Team B's 6 marks, a difference of 1 mark or approximately 10 pins. At that point Team A knows they have about 10 pins more than Team B without looking at scores. At the end of the game Team A has 2 marks more than Team B so they will win by approximately 20 pins.

This system is more commonly used in league bowling since team progress is difficult to figure because of the five different scores. After each complete frame, the scorer adds the total marks to that point of the total team.

Mark Guidelines

- To receive a mark, it is necessary for a player to get a strike or a spare.
- To gain two marks in a frame, it is necessary for a player to get two strikes in a row.

- Four ways of losing marks are:
  1. Following a spare, with the next ball the bowler knocks down fewer than five pins.

  2. Following a strike, the bowler knocks down less than five pins on his/her two attempts.

  3. Following a double, the bowler rolls the next ball and knocks down less than five pins.

  4. Following a double, the bowler knocks down less than five pins total on two ball deliveries.
     Loss of 2 marks.

Figuring Team Handicap Differences into Marks

At the start of the first game, each team finds its handicap. The team handicaps are then compared to determine the pin difference, if any.

Should one team have 6 or more pins handicap than the other, the difference is converted into marks, i.e. the difference is divided by 10. This number of marks is then recorded on the lower left edge of the scoresheet to indicate the advantage one team has at the start of the game.

Cumulative marks are than recorded for each team in each frame to allow the teams to see their competitive progress throughout the game. In this way, a team can tell how far ahead or behind they are at the end of any given frame.

In figuring marks from the handicap, if the figure comes out to a fraction, round if off to the closest number. This is the only time any numbers are rounded off. In all cases of figuring averages and/or handicaps, any extra pins or fractions are dropped.

MARK CHART FOR VARIOUS GAME SCORES

The following chart indicates how many marks (strikes and spares) are normally required to reach different scores. A maximum score of only 90 is possible without making a spare or strike. And, it is impossible to bowl over 200 without having two strikes together.

TO SCORE:	MARKS REQUIRED:
91-103	1
104-113	2
114-123	3
124-133	4
134-143	5
144-153	6
154-163	7
164-173	8
174-183	9
184 & Over	10

ABSENT LEAGUE BOWLER

Each league establishes a "blind score" or "dummy" score in case a member of a team is absent. The most commonly used "blind score" is found by taking the absent bowler's current average minus 10 and that is his/her game score. By using the aforementioned "mark chart," the team may place in "marks" according to the "blind score" in order to keep the mark count accurate.

SETTING UP A LEAGUE SCHEDULE

In setting up a league schedule, the most important factor to consider is to make sure each team gets an equal chance. This is accomplished by making sure the teams rotate lanes each session and that each team gets to roll against all other teams an equal number of times.

Lane assignments can be assigned for the entire league schedule the first day of the league. The following are single round robin schedules for leagues with 6, 8, 10, or 12 teams respectively.

League   **Lane Assignments**   **6 Team Schedule**

Insert Lane Numbers

DATE		TEAM CODE NUMBERS		
1		1-2	3-4	5-6
2		3-5	2-6	1-4
3		1-6	2-3	4-5
4		4-2	1-5	6-3
5		6-4	1-3	5-2

League   **Lane Assignments**   **8 Team Schedule**

Insert Lane Numbers

DATE		TEAM CODE NUMBERS			
1		1-2	3-4	5-6	7-8
2		6-8	5-7	2-4	1-3
3		5-4	1-8	7-3	2-6
4		3-6	7-2	1-5	8-4
5		7-1	4-6	3-8	5-2
6		2-3	8-5	4-1	6-7
7		4-7	6-1	8-2	3-5

League   **Lane Assignments**   **10 Team Schedule**

Insert Lane Numbers

DATE		TEAM CODE NUMBERS				
1		1-2	3-4	5-6	7-8	9-10
2		7-3	1-6	2-9	5-10	8-4
3		4-5	9-8	10-1	3-2	6-7
4		9-1	5-3	4-7	8-6	10-2
5		10-7	6-2	8-3	4-1	5-9
6		5-8	10-4	7-2	6-9	1-3
7		6-4	7-9	1-5	10-3	2-8
8		3-9	8-1	6-10	2-4	7-5
9		8-10	2-5	9-4	1-7	3-6

League   **Lane Assignments**   **12 Team Schedule**

				Insert Lane Numbers	
DATE	TEAM CODE NUMBERS				
1	1-2	3-4	5-6	7-8	9-10	11-12
2	4-5	6-2	12-3	9-11	1-7	10-8
3	9-3	1-10	11-4	5-12	8-2	6-7
4	7-12	5-8	9-2	10-4	11-6	1-3
5	11-8	9-7	1-5	6-3	10-12	2-4
6	10-6	11-1	3-8	12-2	7-4	9-5
7	5-7	4-12	2-10	1-9	6-8	3-11
8	12-9	10-5	7-11	4-6	2-3	8-1
9	6-1	2-11	8-12	3-5	4-9	7-10
10	3-10	8-9	4-1	2-7	5-11	12-6
11	8-4	7-3	6-9	11-10	12-1	5-2

Appendix C

Rules of Bowling

The following is a summary of rules and regulations in the game of bowling as established by the American Bowling Congress and the Women's International Bowling Congress.

- In league play, a team shall start bowling on the lane for which they are scheduled. The team then alternates lanes with the paired lane for each succeeding frame. The second game is started on the paired lane.
- During or after the delivery, if any part of a bowler touches beyond the foul line, it constitutes a foul. Touching a wall, post or other structure, unless local ground rules are established, also constitutes a foul.
- If a bowler fouls on the first ball delivery of a frame, the pins knocked down do not count and all of the pins are reset for the second ball delivery. Only the pins knocked down on the second ball roll count. If a bowler does knock all 10 pins down with the second ball, it is recorded as a spare.
- If a bowler fouls on the second ball of a frame, only the pin count from the first ball roll is recorded.
- Pins knocked down by a ball that first falls into the channel do not count. If this occurs on the first roll of a frame, this pin(s) must be reset before the next ball delivery.
- Pins that are moved off to the side or bounce off the lane and back again, but remain standing, are considered as pins standing. If any standing pin is knocked down by the pinsetter, it must be placed into position before the next ball roll.
- All deadwood (pins knocked down) must be cleared from the lane before the next ball is delivered.

- Pins knocked over by a ball rebounding off the rear cushion do not count.
- In the case of a "dead ball," that ball shall not count and the pins shall be respotted for a rebowl situation. The following are situations where a "dead ball" is declared:

1. There is interference with the ball before it reaches the pins.
2. One or more pins are missing from the set-up.
3. Bowling on the wrong lane or out of turn.
4. When a player is interfered with before the delivery is completed, providing the bowler immediately calls attention to the fact.
5. A pin is interfered with before the ball reaches it.

Appendix D

Novelty Bowling Events

"BEST BALL"

"Best Ball" is a variation of a doubles tournament in which each player rolls. If the first bowler on a team rolls a strike, his/her team has a strike. If he/she fails to get a strike, then the partner gets a try for a strike. If both fail, it goes to a successful spare. If neither pick up the spare, the score for the frame will be the highest pin count of either team member.

"SCOTCH DOUBLES"

"Scotch Doubles" is a type of doubles play in which one partner rolls the first ball of the frame on the even lane, and the other on the odd. If the first ball roll does not result in a strike, the partner shoots for the spare.

A variation of this could be played where the partner alternate shots regardless of the lane.

"LOW BALL"

The object in "Low Ball" is to come out with the lowest score possible. While rolling the ball, competitors must knock at least one pin down with each ball. If this does not occur, the bowler is credited with a strike.

"BINGO BOWLING"

In "Bingo Bowling," only strikes are recorded on a printed bingo card. The bingo card boxes are numbered from 1 through 25 with the center space marked "Free." The bowler will roll 24 balls and fill in the respective space if a strike is rolled. After the final ball is rolled, the X's will show whether the bowler has a "Bingo" . . . a straight or four corners. Prizes are awarded accordingly.

"PROGRESSIVE PIN SHOOT"

There are several variations in "Progressive Pin Shooting", each resulting in an interesting and challenging game.

• Each bowler will roll a ball at a full set of pins on ten different lanes. Each lane has a designated number of pins which each bowler is to knock down on each ball roll. Lane 1 may have one pin limit; lane two a two pin limit, etc. The first person to get through the ten lanes successfully wins.
• The same is done as in #1 but if the bowler fails to knock down the required pins, he/she must start over again.
• Another variation is to merely have the bowlers knock pins down progressively and the person who gets the highest number before missing is the winner. Everyone must knock down one pin on the first ball, two or more pins on the second, three or more on the third, etc.
• The above #3 can also be done in the reverse starting with a strike and working down to a single pin.

"TURKEY SHOOT"

For holiday novelty days such as Thanksgiving, special feats can be rewarded with prizes. Examples of these are:

• Get a turkey
• Roll 3 spares in a row
• Roll 3 splits in a row
• Convert 3 splits in a line
• Score a 111 in the 7th frame.

Appendix E
Glossary of Terms

ALLEY—The sixty feet of pine and maple in front of foul line on which the ball is rolled (more commonly known today as lane).

ANCHOR MAN—The last or fifth man in a team's lineup.

APPROACH—Maple area behind the foul line where bowler executes steps and delivery.

AVERAGE—Figure reached by dividing total sum of game or scores by the number of games bowled in one session or season.

BABY SPLIT—Any split where pins are 12 inches apart, 2-7, 3-10, 4-5, 5-6, 7-8, or 9-10.

BACKUP BALL—A reverse hook; a ball that curves from left to right on the lane (for a right-hander).

BED POST—The 7-10 split.

BIG FOUR—The 4-6-7-10 split.

BLIND SCORE—Score given a team for its absent member.

BLOW—Failure to make a spare; an error, miss.

BOARDS—Individual strips of wood which make up the lane and approach.

BODY ENGLISH—Physical gyrations after the ball has been delivered, as if to steer the ball.

BPAA—The Bowling Proprietors Association of America; association of bowling center operators.

BRIDGE—The distance between the finger holes.

BROOKLYN STRIKE—A ball crossing into the 1-2 pocket resulting in a strike (right-handers).

CHANNEL—Accepted term for the gutter.

CHERRY—To chop; to miss a pin of a two pin spare.

CHOP—Picking a cherry.

CROSSOVER—A ball going to 1-2 pocket side for a right-hander, 1-3 for left-hander.

CURVE—A ball which moves to the left from the moment it is delivered. Not a hook which waits until it nears the pins before breaking to the left.

CUSHION—Barrier at the rear of the pit that absorbs the pins and balls.

DEAD BALL—A ball with very little action; little pin carry.

DEADWOOD—Pins left down on pin deck after the first ball of frame.

DECK—Portion of lane where the pins are set.

DOUBLE—Two consecutive strikes.

DOUBLE PINOCHLE—The 4-6-7-10 set-up.

DUTCH 200—A 200 game scored by rolling alternate frames of spares and strikes.

ERROR—A miss.

FAST—Lanes which hold down the hook; sometimes referred to as "oily", "slick." Today these lanes are more accurately referred to as "holding"

FOUL—The act of going beyond the foul line as you deliver the ball.

FRAME—1/10th of a game.

FULL HIT—A ball that hits squarely on the headpin. Used to describe any ball that hits the target squarely or dead center.

FULL ROLLER—A hook type of release in which the thumb rotates 10-11 o'clock and fingers lift through the ball.

GOAL POSTS—The 7-10 split.

GRAVE YARD—The toughest lanes on which to produce good scores.

GUTTER—Channel or deep grooves on each side of the bowling lane.

HANDICAP—Adjustment in score totals between individuals or teams to equalize competition.

HEADPIN—The number 1 pin.

HIGH HIT, HEAVY HIT—A strike ball that comes into the head pin more than the 3 pin of the 1-3 pocket.

HOOK—A ball that breaks from right to left well after release (for right-handers.)

HOUSE BALL—A ball provided by the bowling center for customer use.

KICKBACK—Side partitions between lanes at pit end.

KING PIN—The 5 pin.

LANE—Sixty-foot maple-pine surface in front of foul line on which ball is rolled; also called alley.

LEADOFF—The first person on a team.

LEAGUE—An organzied group of teams competing on a regular, formal basis under a specific code of rules and regulations.

LEAVE—The pins left standing after the first ball has been rolled.

LIFT—Giving the ball an upward motion with the fingers at point of release.

LIGHT HIT, THIN HIT—Strike ball that fails to come up into the 1-3

pocket; hits more on the 3 pin than the head pin.

LILY—The 5-7-10 split; "sour apple".

LOCATOR DOTS—The 3 rows of dots on the approach.

LOFTING—Throwing the ball out on the lane well beyond the foul line so it drops from a height.

LPBT—Ladies Professional Bowling Tour

MARK—A strike or a spare.

MISS, ERROR, BLOW—Ball not making contact with any pins standing.

MIXER—A good working ball that produces lively action among the pins.

NBC—The National Bowling Council; bowling industry promotion and service organization.

OPEN FRAME—A frame without a strike or spare.

PBA—Professional Bowlers Association; organization of male professional bowlers.

PERFECT STRIKE—A ball that hits the pins squarely in the pocket (between the 1 and 3 pins) and clears the deck of all pins.

PICKET FENCE—The 1-2-4-7 or 1-3-6-10.

PINSPOTTER, PINSETTER—Automatic machine that picks up and sets the pins for the bowler.

PIT—Area at the end of the lane into which the pins fall.

PITCH—The angle in relation to the center of the ball at which the thumb and finger holes of a ball are drilled.

POCKET—The areas between the 1 and 3 pins; the strike zone.

POWERHOUSE—A very strong hooking ball that seems to tear the pins apart.

PUMPKIN—The opposite of powerhouse.

PUSHAWAY—The outward, downward thrust of the ball that puts the ball into motion.

RUNNING LANE—A lane on which the ball hooks quite readily.

SCRATCH—Use of actual scores and averages in individual or team competition; non-handicap bowling.

SEMI-ROLLER—A hook type of release in which the thumb rotates counter-clockwise (11-10 o'clock) and the finger lift throws the ball.

SLEEPER—A hidden pin; the 8 pin in the 2-8 setup.

SLOW LANE—Double meaning term used in describing a lane which either resists a hook or assists it. Varies with geographical areas.

SPAN—The distance between the thumb and finger holes.

SPARE—Knock down all ten pins in one frame with two rolls of the ball.

SPINNER—A method of release that imparts an excessive counter-clock-wise rotation of the thumb (10-7 o'clock).

SPLIT—Two or more pins left standing after the first roll with a pin down immediately between or ahead of them (providing the #1 pin is down also).

SPOT—A target guide on the lane used to aid the bowler in directing his ball; also term used to designate the handicap given another bowler or team.

STRIKE—Knock down all the pins with the first roll of the ball in a frame.

STRIKE OUT—Three consecutive strikes in the tenth frame.

SWEEP—The metal mechanism that cleans the pin deck after each delivery of the ball.

SWEEPER—A wide-breaking hook or curve that seems to "sweep" all the pins into the pit; a strike.

TAP—An apparently perfect strike hit that leaves the 8 pin standing.

TARGET ARROW—Aiming device located on lane approximately 15 feet in front of the foul line. Also called range finder or marks.

TRIPLE—Three strikes in succession. Also a turkey.

TURKEY—Three strikes in a row.

WASHOUT—The 1-2-10 or the 1-2-4-10 spares.

WIBC—Womens International Bowling Congress; an organization of women bowlers.

WOOLWORTH, 5 & DIME—The 5-10 split.

WORKING BALL—Ball that moves with good rolling action, see Mixer.

YABA—Young America Bowling Alliance, an organization sponsoring bowling for youngsters.

Appendix F

Bowler's Analysis Chart (National Bowling Council)

NAME .... LEFT HANDED ☐
                                                                RIGHT HANDED ☐

BALL   **GRIP:** CONVENTIONAL ☐   FINGER TIP ☐
            SEMI-FINGER TIP ☐   OTHER ☐

            SPECS: WEIGHT _____   TOP ☐   SIDE ☐   FINGER ☐
            TRACK: FULL ROLLER ☐   SEMI-ROLLER ☐   SPINNER ☐   OTHER ☐

STANCE

COMMENTS

FEET: STRAIGHT TO INTENDED LINE   YES ☐   NO ☐
CLOSE ☐   FAIRLY CLOSE ☐   APART ☐
TOES TOGETHER ☐   LEFT FOOT AHEAD ☐
RIGHT FOOT AHEAD ☐

WEIGHT DISTRIBUTION: MOSTLY RIGHT ☐
MOSTLY LEFT ☐   EVENLY DISTRIBUTED ☐

KNEES: BOTH BENT ☐   RIGHT BENT ☐
LEFT BENT ☐   STRAIGHT ☐

RELATIVE HEIGHT OF BALL: CHEST HIGH ☐
WAIST HIGH ☐   KNEE HIGH ☐

ALIGNMENT OF BALL: RIGHT OF SHOULDER ☐
IN LINE WITH SHOULDER ☐   AT CENTER LINE ☐
BETWEEN SHOULDER AND CENTER LINE ☐

WEIGHT OF BALL: RIGHT HAND ☐   LEFT HAND ☐
DISTRIBUTED BETWEEN BOTH HANDS ☐

ELBOW: TUCKED INTO HIP ☐   AWAY FROM HIP ☐

WRIST: STRAIGHT ☐   FAIRLY STRAIGHT ☐   BENT ☐

THUMB POSITION: RELATIVE POSITION ON CLOCK _____

APPROACH
COMMENTS

NUMBER OF STEPS _____

LENGTH OF STEPS..LONG ☐   MODERATE ☐   SHORT. ☐

TEMPO ....FAST ☐   MODERATE ☐   SLOW ☐

                 HEEL-TOE ☐   SHUFFLE ☐

                 STRAIGHT ☐   DRIFT RIGHT ☐

                 DRIFT LEFT ☐

ARMSWING: PARALLEL ☐   OUTSIDE-IN ☐   INSIDE-OUT ☐

        LOOP ☐   BENT ELBOW ☐

RIGHT ANGLES TO INTENDED LINE:

SHOULDERS   HIPS

     FACING ⟨ RIGHT —— ☐   FACING ⟨ RIGHT —— ☐
               LEFT —— ☐   LEFT —— ☐

BACKSWING: BELOW WAIST ☐   WAIST HIGH ☐

           AT SHOULDER LEVEL ☐   ABOVE SHOULDER LEVEL ☐

WRIST: FIRM ☐   BENT BACK ☐   CUPPED ☐

BALANCE LINE:GOOD KNEE BEND ☐TOO MUCH ☐ NOT ENOUGH ☐
                 GOOD WAIST BEND ☐   TOO MUCH ☐   NOT ENOUGH ☐

RELEASE
COMMENTS

PALM: DOWN ☐   LEFT ☐   UP ☐   RIGHT ☐

WRIST: FIRM ☐   SAGGED ☐   ROTATES.......LEFT ☐.......RIGHT ☐

FINGERS: FIRM ☐   CLOSED ☐   OPEN ☐

LIFT: SMOOTH ☐   CRISP ☐   WEAK ☐

OUTSIDE FINGERS: BOTH CLOSE ☐   BOTH SPREAD · ☐
                INDEX FINGER SPREAD ☐   LITTLE FINGER SPREAD ☐
                LITTLE FINGER TUCKED UNDER ☐

FOLLOW THROUGH
COMMENTS

DIRECTION RELATIVE TO TARGET:
       IN LINE ☐   RIGHT OF TARGET ☐   LEFT OF TARGET ☐

HEIGHT:
       WAIST ☐   SHOULDER ☐   OVERHEAD ☐   INCONSISTENT ☐

BALL ROLL
COMMENTS

ACTION: STRAIGHT ☐   HOOK ☐   CURVE ☐   BACK-UP ☐
                NUMBER OF BOARDS_____

HITTING POWER: STRONG ☐   WEAK ☐   NORMAL ☐

METHOD OF AIMING
COMMENTS

SPOT: FOUL LINE ☐   LINE

       DOTS .... ☐   PIN ☐   SHADOW ☐   OR ☐

       ARROWS . ☐   AREA

**SPARE
SHOOTING**

COMMENTS

SPOT BOWLER: SPARE TO LEFT
USES STRIKE TARGET – MOVES RIGHT ☐
FOOT PLACEMENT SAME – TARGET MOVED ☐
COMBINATION ☐

SPOT BOWLER: SPARE TO RIGHT
USES THIRD ARROW – MOVES FEET LEFT ☐
FOOT PLACEMENT SAME – TARGET MOVED ☐
COMBINATION ☐

COMMENTS 1st ANALYSIS	2nd ANALYSIS	3rd ANALYSIS	4th ANALYSIS

By knowing the concepts and principles involved in effective movement, learning can be enhanced by making it more meaningful.